AF333152

WHY COMPUTERS ARE COMPUTERS

IN CELEBRATION OF THE

50TH ANNIVERSARY

OF ELECTRONIC COMPUTERS

Also by David Rutland

BEHIND THE FRONT PANEL
The Design & Development of 1920's Radios

Harry D. Huskey and the SWAC

WHY COMPUTERS ARE COMPUTERS

THE SWAC AND THE PC

BY DAVID RUTLAND

With a Foreword by
Harry D. Huskey

Wren
Publishers
PO Box 1084
Philomath, OR 97370

Wren Publishers
PO Box 1084, Philomath, OR 97370

Manufactured in the United States of America

ISBN   1-885391-05-6 (Hardcover)
        1-885391-06-4 (Softcover)

Library of Congress Catalog Card Number: 94-62225

Publishers Catalog-in-Publication Data

Rutland, David
Why Computers Are Computers: the SWAC and the PC / by David
Rutland; with a foreword by Harry D. Huskey

Includes bibliographic references (p.) and index.

1. Electronic digital computers—History.
2. Swac Computer—History I. Title

QA76.8.S8 R8 1995

004.1

Printed on acid-free paper

*For
Crystal and Stacey
Heather and Jason
Greg and Tim
who will inherit
the 21st Century*

CONTENTS

Foreword xi
Preface xiv
1. The Computer 1
2. In England after World War II 6
3. Later in Los Angeles 17
4. The Computer Room 28
5. Counting and Numbers 36
6. The Symposium 43
7. Decisions 49
8. The Stored Program Concept 55
9. Loops within Loops 64
10. What's in a Name? 77
11. Tubes Galore 83
12. Getting Started 92
13. While We Worked 104
14. Making It Work 110
15. The Dedication 121
16. Points of View 128
17. Growing Up 138
18. The SWAC and the PC 146

Appendix 1. The Method of Differences 154
Appendix 2. The SWAC Arithmetic Unit 157
Appendix 3. The SWAC Williams Tube Memory 159
Appendix 4. The SWAC Instruction 162
Chronology 165
Further Reading 168
Index 174

LIST OF ILLUSTRATIONS

Fig. 1   The SWAC and Control Console

Fig. 2   Harry D. Huskey at the Control Console

Fig. 3   The Magnetic Drum and Card Reader/Punch

Fig. 4   The Card Reader/Punches

Fig. 5   The Institute of Numerical Analysis (INA)

Fig. 6   The SWAC Team at Work

Fig. 7   Huskey Examines a Memory Chassis

Fig. 8   Williams Tube's Dots and Dashes

Fig. 9   Ambrosio Checks the Wiring

Fig. 10   The Memory Unit under Construction

Fig. 11   An Arithmetic Unit Rack

Fig. 12   The Arithmetic Unit

Fig. 13   The Two Arithmetic Unit Chassis

Fig. 14   The Memory and Control Racks

Fig. 15   The Control Unit being Tested

Fig. 16   The Magnetic Drum

Fig. 17   SWAC Power Supply

Fig. 18   A Power Distribution Panel

FOREWORD

Although the need for mathematical tables, particularly navigation tables, had long been a driving force in the development of automatic digital computation, it was only with the computer demands of the Second World War that the needs and means culminated in the birth of the electronic digital computer.

Almost a 100 years before, in the 1840's, Charles Babbage, again motivated by the need for navigation tables, designed and tried to construct a special purpose mechanical digital computer, his "Difference Engine." Using the punched-card mechanism of Jacquard's automatic loom, he realized that a computing device could be made to carry out any arbitrary sequence of arithmetic operations, including conditional sequences that were dependent on values computed by the machine. It was this feature that he incorporated in his final machine, the "Analytical Engine." However, the means was not there — neither financial nor technological! Not having completed the Difference Engine, Babbage failed to obtain government support for building the Analytical Engine. Hand-making a few gears for a clock was in reach of nineteenth century technology, but that was orders of magnitude simpler than making the multitude of precision gears needed for the Analytical Engine.

The development of electrical punched-card machines, starting with Hollerith in 1890, gave the means for Howard Aiken of Harvard University, working with IBM, to build a modern version of Babbage's Analytical Engine early in World War II. During the war, Bell Telephone Laboratories developed general purpose digital computers and, unknown to the rest of the world, Konrad Zuse in Germany was also developing digital computers. At Iowa State University, J. V. Atanasoff built a prototype of an electronic digital special purpose computer to solve systems of linear equations. His machine was unique as it used electrical capacitors to store binary numbers. In England, a code-breaking team, including Alan Turing, constructed a special purpose electronic computer, the "Colossus." Turing went on after World War II to design and construct a general purpose computer that was called, after Babbage, the "Automatic Computing Engine," or ACE.

The need for gunner's firing tables during the war led the U. S. Army Ordnance Department to support J. Presper Eckert and John Mauchly in building a general purpose electronic digital computer—the ENIAC—optimized for calculating the firing tables. Although the ENIAC had 18,000 vacuum tubes, it could store only 20 10 digit numbers. Driven by the need to store many more numbers, Eckert and Mauchly looked for physical phenomena that could be used to store information. Mercury delay lines used in range measurements in radar offered one possibility. A five foot pipe filled with mercury could store an arbitrary sequence of 1000 pulses, which could be the equivalent of 32 10 decimal-digit numbers. Contrast the less than a dozen tubes used by this new electronic "memory" with the many required by the ENIAC.

In England, this need for storing large amounts of information and his experience with the detection of moving radar targets led Fred Williams to develop CRT's (Television-like tubes) for storage.

With numbers being available in a few microseconds in both mercury lines and CRT's, how did one supply the control information specifying the sequence of arithmetic steps? The plug-panel wiring used in the ENIAC was fast enough but inflexible. Instructions stored as holes in punched-paper tape took milliseconds (1000's of microseconds) to read. The obvious way was to store the instructions on the mercury lines or the CRT's like the numbers and they could then be available at the same rate. Thus the modern stored program automatic digital computer was conceived.

This is the background to this book. At the end of World

War II no one was sure which memory would work best. The only logical device was a simple two-input "AND" gate, a multiple grid vacuum tube. At each logical element the signals changed by 100 volts! Crystal diodes and integrated circuits were still in the future.

This book tells the story of a small group of people who, in the environment I have just described, built a computer which was the fastest in existence at the time of its dedication in 1950.

Harry D. Huskey
Professor Emeritus
Information Sciences
University of California at Santa Cruz
January 1995

PREFACE

This book is about computers. But it does not tell how a modern personal computer works or how to use a software package. If you wish to learn how to work your own computer, you won't find the answers here. But if you would like to know what basic principles lie behind the keyboard and video screen of your computer—the same basic principles of all computers since they were invented 50 years ago—then I have written this book for you.

As someone who was able to work on the early computers, I have seen the computer gradually and steadily become involved in everyone's daily life. Yet it seems that the basic invention that made the computer possible remains a mystery to everyone except the experts. Now, as we approach the 50th anniversary of the first electronic general purpose computer, the ENIAC, I would like to remedy this situation. I have therefore attempted to give an easily understandable explanation of what every one of today's computers has in common, what makes them able to help us in so many ways and why they're unlike any other machine. In doing so, I have used the history of one of the first digital computers to describe what makes a computer a computer.

So I have written the story of this great computer invention, the "Stored Program Concept," and the men who invented it. I also tell the story of the SWAC, one of the early computers, and the men who were responsible for its design and construction. I have relied on the many computer historians who have over the years written so many books and articles on the history of computers. These have supplied me basic facts and figures and I am grateful to be able to list them in the section on "Further Reading."

I thank those who have supplied me further details on the SWAC. The man responsible for the SWAC construction, Dr. Harry Huskey, has kindly provided many of the photographs and has reviewed my manuscript. My book incorporates many of his thoughts and suggestions. Mr. Biagio Ambrosio, who worked with me as one of the SWAC engineers, has contributed more photographs and his reminiscences. In addition, Mr. Kevin Corbitt of the Charles Babbage Institute, has been very helpful. Finally, thanks go out to the Oregon State University Library and the anonymous librarians that helped me find answers to my obscure questions.

I know I would not have finished writing this book without my family and friends who gave me the needed encouragement.

David Rutland
January 1995

WHY COMPUTERS ARE COMPUTERS

IN CELEBRATION OF THE
50TH ANNIVERSARY
OF THE COMPUTER

THE COMPUTER

The digital computer so permeates our lives today that it seems unnecessary to have to point it out. Yet still it needs to be emphasized so we don't forget that many of us can remember a world without the computer. It is hard for the younger generation to even conceive how people survived in those days without the modern technological gadgets that fill our homes. These "marvels of technology," as they are referred to repeatedly in the popular press, not only include the computer, but also color television and the VCR, stereo hi-fi's, immediate long distance telephone and TV via satellite and the microwave oven. But putting all these in one class is, in my mind, a serious error. The digital computer is definitely in a class by itself. The computer is a machine that is infinitely flexible. When you buy a computer, the advice that a knowledgeable "expert" should, and most often gives, is to choose the computer that has the right "software," that incomprehensible stuff that comes on floppy disks. The floppy disk is not software; it's real and solid "hardware," but the coded information and instructions is the software. It's the software that makes the computer have it's flexibility so that it is now a necessary and indispensable tool for almost everything we do in life. There's the personal computer, the ubiquitous "PC" on everyone's desk at home, in the office and in the smallest business. Each personal computer looks much the same from the outside, having only slight variations in cabinet style. They are also much the same inside with the solid-state integrated circuits arranged in a configuration that hasn't changed since the computer was invented. If they look the same and have the same basic configuration, how is it that each one can do so many jobs? Of course we all know it's the "software" that can make our computer at one time a word processor, another time an accounting machine, an appointment calendar or even run a complicated production line. If we raise our sights and look at what other computers are doing, we see them flying the Space Shuttle, calculating the position of the stars and solving advanced mathematical problems that couldn't be solved before. Just plug in another floppy-disc with some different software and your computer has turned into a new machine, interacting differently with you and solving entirely different problems. This is why the computer is unlike the other technological "gadgets" that we see and use everyday. Can you, merely by doing something as simple as plugging in a floppy disk, change your VCR into a stereo system, your toaster into a refrigerator or your car into a truck? Each of these machines does one and only one thing and cannot be changed unless an engineer builds a new one from the "ground up." But you can change your computer in a few seconds from one application to another, and we are so used to it we tend to take it for granted.

In a short while, all those interested in computers will be celebrating the 50th anniversary of the first electronic general-purpose digital computer, the ENIAC. In November, 1945 not only was the ENIAC completed, but those involved with its construction had already invented the computer as we know it, the flexible machine ready to help you in an infinite number of ways. This invention surely ranks high among the great inventions of history. We all know the names Thomas Alva Edison, Alexander Graham Bell, and even Eliah Whitney, the inventor of the cotton gin. Yet the names of those who have influenced our lives as much or more than these great men are lost in history. These men were John von Neumann, J. Presper Eckert and John Mauchly. Their invention is called the "Stored Program Concept." Without it we would not have had the computer revolution that took place in the last 50 years. Our personal computers are stored-program computers, just like all the electronic digital computers since the ENIAC. The Stored Program Concept is so important and has had such an influence on all our lives that it is imperative for everyone to understand it. There are now many hundreds of books claiming to make it easy for you to "understand" your computer. Most deal with the details of operating a particular software program. Others describe the integrated circuit electronics in technical jargon that only someone familiar with computer technology can understand. Yet the basic principles of a computer are the same now as they were 50 years ago and can be understood by anyone who knows how to add and multiply.

Computers do what humans did when they first used stones for counting and later on made the abacus and mechanical calculator. Yes, computers are much faster, but they are not just fancier calculators. Their power comes from their ability to make decisions. When using an adding machine, it's your intelligence that decides which numbers to enter and whether you should add, subtract, multiply and so on. You make the decisions, the calculator doesn't. Using the Stored Program Concept, the computer combines the calculating power of the mechanical calculator with the decision making power of the human brain to produce the device that we know today.

An early stored program computer was the first computer built on the West Coast of the United States. When it was completed in 1950, it was the fastest computer in the world. Built by the National Bureau of Standards on the campus of the University of California at Los Angeles (UCLA), it was given the name, "National Bureau of Standards Western Automatic Computer," or SWAC for short. The SWAC was designed and constructed by one of the early pioneers that had worked with the ENIAC, Dr. Harry D. Huskey. It was Huskey's concept and Huskey's will that produced the SWAC.

Not only was the SWAC an important machine in the history of computers, but its organization and operating principles were very similar to that of your personal computer. On the other hand its physical appearance was very different. Your computer is light enough for you to carry, while the SWAC and its auxiliary equipment weighed over a ton. Your computer will fit on or near your desk, the SWAC occupied a whole room and more. But if you could have looked behind its physical appearance, you would have found that the SWAC had all the elements of your computer and operated in the same way. Your computer is a stored program computer. The SWAC was a stored program computer. Your computer has an internal "clock," a memory and an arithmetic logic unit consisting of a control and arithmetic unit. The SWAC had all these same units. It even had a keyboard for the operator to enter problems. Although the TV screen display we have today was not yet invented, the SWAC typed out results on an electric typewriter. The SWAC was not as fast or powerful as your personal computer, but it had all the basic hardware elements and its software operated in the same basic fashion.

The importance of the Stored Program Concept and the similarity of the SWAC to today's computers are the two themes of this book. You don't have to be a computer expert to understand them and I won't confuse you with computer-ese. The history of the SWAC and how it was produced is a fascinating story of hard-headed computer pioneers, the "accidents" of history and the people that put it together. I was part of the team of engineers that built the SWAC and was fortunate to experience first-hand the excitement of the times when the first computers were built.

Although the SWAC story takes place in the United States and more specifically in Los Angeles, its story starts across the ocean in England. Here, after the war, we find the English trying to catch up with, and at times surpassing, the computer developments in the States.

IN ENGLAND AFTER WORLD WAR II

In December 1946, only a little more than a year after the VJ day and the end of the World War, England was still feeling the effect of the German blockade. Everything was in short supply and rationing of most civilian essentials was still on. No one had more than one egg and a small amount of meat each week. To the young mathematician and his wife and two young daughters who had just arrived from America things seemed meager to the extreme. He had brought a small supply of canned corned beef with him and then found that corned beef from Australia was the only meat one could buy without ration coupons. So they rapidly grew tired of a corned beef diet.

He was here at the request of England's National Physical Laboratory (NPL) to help in the formation of their program to build the first digital computer in England. He was hired as one of the few "computer experts" who obtained their computer experience with the first digital computer, the ENIAC, at the Moore School of Engineering at the University of Pennsylvania. His salary was to be the equivalent of $5000 a year, a good salary at that time for a mathematics PhD with only a few years out of school.

At the time of his arrival in England, Dr. Harry Huskey could not have foreseen that he was destined to be in a few years the builder of the very first computer in the western United States. His career was even harder to predict when as a young boy in the 1920's his father moved the family from his birthplace, Bryson City, North Carolina, to seek his fortune on an Idaho farm near Pocatello. Huskey completed high school in Pocatello and went on to study mathematics at the University of Idaho in Moscow, Idaho. After getting the B. S. degree in mathematics he enrolled as a graduate student at Ohio State University to obtain his doctorate degree in mathematics in early 1943.

In July 1943, three years before his trip to England, Huskey joined the faculty of the University of Pennsylvania. Besides his teaching assignments he became involved with the University's Moore School of Engineering. Here the first electronic computer, the ENIAC, was being constructed and he was asked to prepare problems to be run on the machine. The ENIAC was programmed by plugging hundreds of wires into a plug board which meant that Huskey not only had to know the mathematics of the problem but also needed to know how the hardware operated. In the course of his experience with the ENIAC Huskey made an analysis of the accuracy of digital numerical calculations which he later published. Although one thinks of a mathematician as one solely interested in esoteric mathematical theory, Huskey was also interested in electronic engineering. In fact he had tried to take a course in radio engineering as an undergraduate at the University of Idaho but lacked the pre-requisites for admission. He therefore had to pursue his interest in electric circuits by taking it upon himself to study the Radiation Laboratory textbooks. These textbooks were the result of the work done by the Massachusetts Institute of Technology (MIT) on the wartime development of radar. In the closing years of the war they were the only definite treatise on what we now call electronic engineering and introduced the student to the latest electronic circuits. As a result of his self-taught electronics, when Huskey was programming the ENIAC to perform his mathematical research problems he took a serious interest in both the mathematical and electronic engineering aspects of the computer, what we would now call software and hardware. This experience culminated in the early months of 1946 with him working on the technical manual for the ENIAC.

The ENIAC was the brainchild of J. Presper Eckert, Jr. and John Mauchly who we will meet again in a later chapter. By March 1946 they had both resigned from the ENIAC project and left the Moore School to start their own computer company. That left the ENIAC project without a leader. The next most experienced scientist on the project was Harry Huskey and the Moore School asked him to assume the position of leader. However, the Mathematics Department of the University had a different idea and didn't want Huskey to leave the Mathematics Department. They pressured the Moore School to find someone else and they withdrew their offer. Huskey felt this decision was unfair to him and in June he resigned from the University of Pennsylvania and sought a position elsewhere.

In the spring of 1946 Professor Douglas R. Hartree of Cambridge University was on a visit to the Moore School. Hartree was already a computer expert in his own right.

He had begun his interest in computers by constructing, in the early 1930's, a mechanical analog machine, the Differential Analyzer, at Manchester University. He had come to the United States to use the ENIAC for a test on a new method of solving certain equations that were important to both mathematicians and physicists. Mathematicians had been unable to find a mathematical solution to these "two-point boundary value problems" and the only solution was to be found by numerical calculations. These calculations involved so many arithmetical operations that it was impractical to compute by hand and hence the speed of the ENIAC opened up the possibility of solutions for the first time. Huskey was completing his work on the accuracy of digital computations known as "round-off errors" at the same time as Hartree's visit and they came to know each other. Huskey, wondering what he was going to do after his stint at the ENIAC, asked Hartree if there might be a possibility of a job in England. Hartree wasn't sure but said he would look into it.

Later in July and August 1946 the Moore school gave a series of lectures entitled "Theory and Techniques for the Design of Electronic Computers". This course was the first of its kind, the first course ever in the world on electronic digital computers. It was therefore attended by mathematicians and engineers from all over the world including Hartree. Another attendant from overseas was Maurice Wilkes of Cambridge University whom Huskey would eventually meet in England. Huskey found himself unable to attend these lectures as in June he had left the University of Pennsylvania and spent that summer as an Instructor in mathematics at his alma mater Ohio State. His duties involved the teaching of mathematics in an extension program at Wright-Paterson Air Force Base. In July he was pleasantly surprised to receive a cable offering him the job in England at the National Physical Laboratory (NPL). This offer came about in part by his acquaintance with Hartree. Neither he, nor his wife, knew what or where NPL was and yet in June he accepted. He immediately applied for passage to England via ship. Even ship travel was limited to VIP's and he had to wait until December before leaving with his family.

They arrived in London in early January 1947, and found that NPL had obtained a room for them at Mrs. Penberthy's boardinghouse. They all had to squeeze into one large room which, like most rooms for rent in England at that time, was heated by one small gas heater. These heaters were made to accept shillings, a coin like our quarter, and they didn't burn very long before another shilling had to be inserted in the slot. It was a cold winter that year, one of the coldest for many years, and to get any heat at all, the heater really "burned" shillings at a high rate.

They learned to sleep in their long underwear and were glad after a month to find a rental house. But the owner returned in six months and they had to find another place to end up their one year stay. Huskey describes their new house in Teddington as "a fairy tale place for us". It was called "The Cottage" and located in London's famous Bushy Park next door to Hampton Court Palace. The headquarters of NPL was close by Bushy House which was also the home of the director, Sir Charles Darwin, the grandson of the great Charles Darwin. The Cottage belonged to the Royal Family and was assigned to Queen Mary's retired secretary. Such places were called "Grace and Favour" establishments and were regularly given to retired servants of the crown to live in for life. It was beautifully furnished with period pieces that were gifts from Queen Mary. There were also presents received by the Queen on her trip to China and a large cabinet full of chinaware from the East India Company. Autographed photographs of the royal family hung in the upstairs hallway and the Queen's deer roamed in the park beyond the garden wall. They rented the front part of the house while the secretary lived in back.

It was now only a short walk for Huskey to go to work which was just as well as he couldn't buy a car in England and had to rely on bicycles and public transportation. All in all the Huskey's had a good time once they settled down. They even bought a motorcycle and side car and toured England and then across the channel to Switzerland. However gas for personal use was banned in the fall and they couldn't sell their motorcycle but gave it to the Queen's Secretary for the last month's rent.

The famous mathematician, Alan Turing, was pioneering the computer work at NPL. By the use of an ingenious special-purpose vacuum tube computer he was part of a team that had broken the German's Enigma code during the war. The allies were then able to read the German radio messages sent to their submarines in the Atlantic. These messages gave away the submarines' positions allowing the allies to route the ship convoys away from danger. Many thousands of lives were saved by Turing and his team working in a small laboratory in England with their special purpose electronic computer that they called the "Colossus". At the end of the World War in October 1945 Turing joined the Mathematics Division at NPL and started design on an all electronic computer.

Huskey's job was to join Turing and his group and help in the design and construction of the new machine which was later named the ACE, the Automatic Computing Engine. By the time Huskey arrived Turing had made as many as five logical designs for the ACE and yet no work had been started on its construction. This was partly due to the lack of a good administrator for the project and partly because Turing had such little interest in the nuts and bolts of electrical engineering. Huskey, on the other hand, with his knowledge of both hardware and software, was eager to become involved in the construction of the computer and pushed for it to begin. It turned out that he and one other member of the team were the only ones with any practical experience in vacuum tube computer circuits.

The first job was to decide which of the five designs to build and Turing was already busy making a sixth design, one he considered an improvement on all the others. These designs were based more on logical diagrams rather than practical computer circuits and therefore were not directly translatable into hardware. Yet the designs represented a novel approach to an electronic computer quite different from those we have today. One would, of course, expect unique and interesting ideas from the man who is now credited with the first mathematical paper describing the problem solving capabilities of a computing machine. His paper had the long mathematical title "On Computable Numbers with an Application to the Entschiedungsproblem" which doesn't sound much like anything to do with computers. But when it was published as early as 1936 in the Proceedings of the London Mathematical Society automatic computing was just a dream. Even so Turing envisioned a universal computing machine and used its theoretical operation to find the solution to this important problem in mathematics. In the course of solving this problem he demonstrated that a machine could be made to solve all problems that could be stated in mathematics. His imaginary machine, among other not too practical devices, required infinite lengths of punched paper tape and certainly was not intended to result in a practical computer. It's no wonder that such a brilliant mathematician could never stop inventing more and more improved designs for the new computer.

Turing wanted to proceed straight away with the construction of the full size ACE and yet, with the resources at hand, Huskey suggested that a small test portion be made first. This "Test Assembly" would prove the electronic circuits needed to implement Turing's design. It seems that Turing and Huskey seriously disagreed about this approach. Turing was very anxious to concentrate on the big "final" machine and didn't want to see effort diverted from that task. At this time Turing was delivering a series of lectures in London and Huskey and other co-workers accompanied him on the train. During this short trip they discussed their diverging views on how the project should proceed. At times they had what their co-workers described as such fierce arguments that they thought they would come to blows. But these were no more then heated "discussions" that were enjoyed by the two mathematicians. On one of these trips Huskey relates that the point in question was still not resolved by the time they had arrived. So Turing's mind was still wrapped up with Huskey's arguments and he had difficulty in concentrating on his lecture.

Eventually Huskey's plan was approved and during the summer of 1947 he and the rest of the personnel turned their full attention to the construction of the Test Assembly. Turing continued to concentrate on his "big" design.

In addition to helping supervise the project during his stay at NPL, Huskey was asked to review the embryonic computer projects in England. He visited Cambridge and Manchester Universities which had computer projects going of their own. He wrote a detailed report on the design and expected performance of these machines. He compared them with similar projects back home at the Moore School and his experience at the ENIAC. In this way in the course of a year he became well acquainted with all the computer projects, both from the viewpoint of the mathematician but also that of the engineer. He studied the designs and methods of construction and compared one with another. This enabled him to weigh in his mind the advantages and disadvantages of the different designs, the engineering difficulties in designing the different electronic memories and the ease or difficulty with which problems could be programmed. This experience made him one of the few experts in digital computing at that time, a valuable addition to any computer organization.

Unfortunately Huskey's time in England was too short to complete the Test Assembly and when he left the project faltered for a while. Yet it gained momentum when the project was transferred from the Mathematics Division to the Radio Division and the full ACE was finally completed in 1951.

While at NPL Huskey had accepted an offer from the U.S. National Bureau of Standards (NBS) (NBS is now called the National Institute of Standards and Technology). His job was to be Chief of the Machine Development Laboratory of the Applied Mathematics Division. He had been offered an important post commeasurate with his experience and he quickly accepted, pleased to have a job to go to on his return to the U.S. Later he received an offer to work on the EDSAC computer project at Cambridge University. Maurice Wilkes, who was in charge of the project, had known of Huskey's work on the ENIAC and at NPL. His desire to have Huskey work on his project underscored his respect for Huskey's abilities and knowledge of computer design. This respect for Huskey is shown by the following quotation from Wilkes' book, *Memoirs of a Computer Pioneer:*

> I got to know Huskey quite well and I realized what a tower of strength he would be if I could persuade him to join the EDSAC project. . .[but] he was not able to accept my offer. . .I have often wondered what difference it would have made to the early history of the subject [computer history] if Huskey's energies and abilities had been applied to the EDSAC instead of the SWAC.

Huskey was tempted to remain in England. But Wilkes' offer had come too late. With his prior acceptance of the position at NBS he had no choice but to return to the United States. Thus we see the effect of chance events having an important effect on the course of the history of computers. If Huskey had not been so quick to accept the NBS offer he may not have returned to the U.S. and the story of the SWAC might never have been written.

Huskey had a memorable year in England and he and his family were sad to leave as they had made many good friends. One of these whose work was a great influence on him later was F.C. Williams of Manchester University where the computer memory system named after him, the Williams tube, was developed. Huskey was later to use the Williams tube for the SWAC memory in quite a different way than that used by Williams. This introduced design problems that took much of Huskey's time. Later, after the SWAC was completed, he had the opportunity to design a Turing type computer for the Bendix Corporation. In his article "From ACE to the G-15," he wrote that "my struggles with the Williams tubes left little time to think about Turing computers".

As he left England he must have been looking forward to his new job as he had been promised that he would be posted to NBS's new Institute for Numerical Analysis (INA) at UCLA in sunny southern California. But first he was to report to NBS in Washington DC where, unknown to him at the time, decisions were going to be made that would give him the opportunity of a lifetime — the construction of the SWAC, fastest of the pioneering computers, a true forerunner of today's personal computer.

3
LATER IN LOS ANGELES

While Harry Huskey was working on the ACE in England, events of a different nature that would eventually bring him and myself together were taking place in Los Angeles. There, the war had not brought the devastation and shortages Huskey found in London, but, quite the contrary, LA was booming. The large aircraft companies like Douglas, Lockheed and North American Aviation had been going full blast during the war and continued to prosper as the Cold War began. As a young engineer completing graduate work at Cal Tech, I spent my summers working at the Aerophysics Laboratory of North American Aviation.

Aerophysics occupied an old lofting room in the attic of the main plant which was located on the eastern edge of what is now LAX, the Los Angeles International Airport. In those days the LA airport was located at the Lockheed Terminal in San Fernando Valley. The present airport was then called Mines Field and was devoted to private aviation and a few aircraft companies of which North American was the biggest. It was here that the famous P-51 Mustang fighter planes were produced by the thousands during World War II.

The events leading up to the formation of the Aerophysics Laboratory really started way back in 1937 when Hitler set up a rocket research center and test station in Peenemunde, Germany, on the Baltic Sea. Dr. Werner Von Braun directed the operations and contributed to the design and production of the V-1 buzz-bomb and the V-2 missile, both used to bomb London. When the Russians invaded Germany at the close of the war, Von Braun and his development team, over 130 scientists and engineers, fled to the West. They, fortunately for the allies, found the U.S. 7th Army and surrendered to them on May 2, 1945. When they were debriefed, they astonished the Americans with far-fetched stories of satellites circling the earth and rockets going to the moon. They brought home in no uncertain terms how really behind we were in rocket development.

After the war, North American set up the Aerophysics Lab under contract with the Air Force to develop a long range missile. Von Braun and his scientists were locked up as prisoners of war at Fort Bliss near El Paso. Of course, the fact that we were thinking of building a long range nuclear missile was highly confidential. This prevented open discussions with the German scientists, the only ones who had built working rockets, because as prisoners of war, they couldn't get the required clearance! However, in 1946, the bureaucracy relented and Von Braun was allowed to oversee the launchings of captured V-2 missiles at the White Sands proving ground. He now has a place in the history books as an American hero for his part in the development of the Saturn 5 moon rocket. That's quite a change from helping Hitler destroy London and it stands as a great credit to all Americans that we can forgive our enemies so easily.

The Aerophysics Lab was staffed with scientists and engineers from all parts of the country. They were recruited, given high salaries and moved at company expense to Los Angeles. North American was only one of many companies to search the whole country for talented technical people. Most of the personnel were new to Los Angeles and "Old-timers" like myself that had grown up in Los Angeles made up the minority. The westward migration to Los Angeles had just begun. So many came that Bob Hope joked that a Native Californian was the guy who just got off the train in front of you!

This influx of scientists to a down to earth airplane factory shook the organization to its very roots. The old practical engineers saw all of us upstairs in the loft as egghead scientists working on "new-fangled" rockets. The factory worked punctual hours and some of the scientists, who were used to the more relaxed hours of the university, got into trouble by punching the time clock at irregular hours. This not only disturbed the payroll system, which docked your pay if you were more than 6 minutes late or left 6 minutes early, but was in flagrant violation of those holier than holy rules known as company policy. In the end the management had to change the policy to prevent the loss of the many scientists that the company had gone to such expense to assemble.

By the summer of 1948, the project had expanded to where the hangar loft wasn't large enough and Aerospace moved out to Downey in East Los Angeles. The Laboratory occupied the old Vought Aircraft plant and later developed into the Aeroneutronics Division of Rockwell International. Aerospace was extremely interested in the development of digital guidance systems for the missiles. The analog electro-mechanical guidance systems had their accuracy limited by the precision that individual components could be manufactured. Since digital systems work with numbers, their precision can be increased merely by adding more decimal places. My job was to apply the new digital techniques to guidance problems and design the necessary digital circuits.

Then, one day in late 1948, an engineer friend of mine said, "Say, David why don't you go out to UCLA and get a job with the new computer project there?". He knew that the thirty mile trip to Downey in East Los Angeles from my house across town was becoming a strain. There was only one freeway in the Los Angeles area in those days, the short Pasadena freeway, and it didn't go in the right direction, so I car pooled it from one end of Manchester Boulevard to the other, taking an hour each way. My friend knew that I was fortunate to be one of only a few engineers that had digital circuit design experience in Southern California, so it seemed that I might have a good chance to land a job with Huskey and work closer to home. Thus, I made plans to go to the Institute of Numerical Analysis (INA) and apply for the job.

Earlier, in January 1948, while I was still at Aerospace, Huskey had returned from England and on February 1 reported to Bureau of Standards in Washington D.C. to await his assignment to INA. The events that started NBS in the computing business and led up to the formation of the INA start before World War II. During the depression many unemployed workers were given jobs by the Works Project Administration (WPA). In 1938, the WPA established the Mathematical Tables Project in New York, which was put under the scientific control of NBS. Here the unemployed were trained to use mechanical calculators to produce mathematical tables.

In mathematics, a table is a list of values of a mathematical equation, or more exactly, a mathematical function. A multiplication table is a simple example which lists the values of the function x times y, usually for the integers 1 through 9, although, as a schoolboy in England, I learned the table from 1 to 12, since there were 12 pennies in a shilling back then. Tables have been used in computations since the earliest days of the Egyptians and Babylonians, thousands of years B.C. Some tables are lists of the positions of stars and planets which historically were important for observing religious rites and for the practice of astrology. Later on, accurate astronomical tables came into importance for sailors to use for navigation. Now they have been replaced with navigation satellites. Before computers, tables of the trigonometric functions, sines, cosines, etc., and those of logarithms, the great aid to multiplying and dividing, were widely used by engineers and surveyors. Before the advent of the laser surveying instruments and their built-in computers, every surveyor carried a handbook of tables. Mathematical tables, like weights and measures, had to be accurate to be useful to the citizens of the country. It was therefore only fitting and proper for the National Bureau of Standards to produce tables that everyone could rely on.

After the war, E. U. Condon became director of NBS and he realized that the new computers would permit the solution of numerical problems at "hitherto undreamed of speeds." He saw the need for a national computer center to provide both consulting and computational services, so he set up the National Applied Mathematics Laboratories (NAML) in 1947 with Dr. John Curtiss as chief. NAML consisted of four major units:

1. The Institute for Numerical Analysis (INA) located at UCLA in April 1948.
2. The Computation Laboratory located in New York and Washington. This took over the operations of the Mathematical Tables Project with their human computers.
3. Statistical Engineering Laboratory to provide consulting services to scientists.
4. Machine Development Laboratory which was to aid in the development of computers and later, in cooperation with the Electronics Division, produced the SEAC.

NAML was soon approached by the Census Bureau to advise them on the feasibility of constructing an electronic computer for tabulating the 1950 census. At that time, the ENIAC was the only working electronic computer, so there was great uncertainty not only as to whether a computer could be made to work, but whether it could be built in time for the census. Toward this end two study contracts were issued. One went to the ENIAC engineers, Eckert and Mauchly, who were now in business on their own. The other contract went to the Raytheon Corporation, a manufacturer of electronic equipment and for the Navy. These reports were submitted in late 1947 to a committee for evaluating the design studies.

In January 1948, Huskey returned from his one year in England at NPL to take up his duties at NAML. He had been told that after about six weeks in Washington he would be taking up his permanent position at INA at UCLA.

However, as it happened, it would not be until the end of that year that he would be sent to Los Angeles. When Huskey reported to work in Washington, the NBS committee had not yet evaluated the design proposals for the Census Bureau. The committee made its report in April. Doubting whether any of the proposed machines could be built in reasonable time, they recommended that NBS start a program to evaluate components for use in digital computers. At about the same time Huskey proposed to Curtiss for NBS to construct an "interim" computer and the decision to do so was reached on May 18, 1948. This machine was built in Washington and became known as the SEAC.

That summer, in anticipation of moving to Los Angeles, the Huskey's came out to California to look for housing. After seeing many houses, they found a home that they liked in Westwood. But as things were still uncertain back at NBS they dared not put a down payment on it. When December came and they were permanently assigned to the INA they had lost all hope of finding this same house. The post war influx of people to Southern California had made housing very short and they were prepared to begin their search all over again. But when they visited the house, they found that it was indeed available and lost no time in buying it.

On the 19th of October, it seemed like there was little progress on the SEAC and there were problems in making its memory work. So a meeting of the Applied Mathematics Executive Council of NBS was called to discuss the situation. Among those who attended were:

John Curtiss, Chief of NAML

Herman Goldstine, Institute of Advanced Study, Princeton

Samuel Alexander, Director of the SEAC project

Mina Rees, Mathematics Branch, Office of Naval
    Research
Sam Feldman, Office of Naval Research
E. W. Cannon, Chief, Machine Development
    Laboratory
Oscar Maier, Air Material Command, Wright Field
L. M. K. Boelter, Dean of Engineering at UCLA
Harry Huskey, Head of Machine Development, INA

They reviewed the status of the computer projects that were then under way. Although there were altogether about 10 projects, none of them seemed to be near completion and many had problems with the construction of their memories. Some were using magnetic drums, the forerunners of today's hard disks, while others were planning to use special tubes that were being developed for computer memories. Still others, like Eckert and Mauchly, were working on the acoustic delay line memories which we will encounter in Chapter 8. None of them were planning to use the Williams tube memory that F. C. Williams was developing in England. The Bureau of Census was still seeking NAML's advice on who should supply them with a computer. The technical people disagreed as to which design would be successful, each one defending the viability of his own project.

Mina Rees said that it was necessary to explore all avenues to supply the immediate need and they should support other groups that were already carrying on computer development. So John Curtiss put forward a proposal to contract for two more machines in addition to the SEAC. One of these would be built by Raytheon and the other by Engineering Research Associates. Since neither of these machines used the Williams tube memory, Curtiss suggested that any money left over in their budget should be spent on research and development of the Williams tube at the Institute for Numerical Analysis at UCLA. Sam Feldman then expressed his reluctance to build any more machines and was very much against starting three new projects. So Mina Rees proposed a compromise for them to contract only for the Raytheon machine and put the rest of the money into building a new machine at INA. This machine would use Williams tubes and be under the direction of Dean Boelter and Huskey. During his one year in England, Huskey already knew of Williams' work and was therefore well qualified to direct the new project. Oscar Maier suggested that the Air Material Command and Office of Naval Research pool their research funds to build the two machines, one at Raytheon and one at INA. The Air Material Command was already supporting other computer projects that did not plan to use Williams tubes so Maier was in favor of the construction of an entirely different kind of machine.

Finally, late in the afternoon it was decided to follow Mina Rees' suggestion and contract for the Raytheon computer and build another machine at INA. This machine was in addition to the SEAC that NBS had already undertaken and was to explore the use of different designs. The design, as we shall see, was to be parallel rather than serial and the memory was to use Williams tubes. In addition, it was important that the construction should proceed speedily so that these machines could be evaluated as to their performance as soon as possible.

Huskey had been handed a difficult assignment. Not only was he going to build a computer unlike any other, but he was under pressure to do it quickly despite the fact that he had no existing engineering staff or production group, nor did he have the space at INA to build it. But it was his chance to build a computer of his own design where he could be his own boss. It was a chance of a lifetime, his own computer in sunny California.

Huskey picked up his family and moved again, the fourth time in less than four years, and started hiring his staff. The administrative tasks, including payroll and the purchasing of supplies, were handled by Al Cohn, INA's administrative officer, which enabled Huskey to put his full attention on the design of the computer. Dean Boelter was enthusiastic about the project and the word quickly spread around the UCLA Engineering Department that an exciting new advanced project was getting underway on campus. In this way, engineers like myself found our way to INA to apply for a job.

One of these engineers was Ed Lacey who was working on anti-submarine sonar systems at the Naval Electronics Laboratory in San Diego. He was hired and upon his return to San Diego told his friend Biagio Ambrosio about the SWAC project and asked him to work with him at INA. Ambrosio had been an engineer at IBM for many years and had worked on their early vacuum tube multiplier and other computer related projects. Both of these men were senior engineers who had been in the migration of skilled people to the Los Angeles area, the same migration that filled the loft at Aerophysics. They knew each other from early days at technical school and they both received their degrees in engineering in the early 1930's, Ambrosio from the University of Michigan and Lacey from Texas A & M. They brought their long engineering experience in the design and construction of electronic equipment to the SWAC. Their practical knowledge of how vacuum tube equipment should be properly built made sure that the SWAC was constructed to have a long life.

Ambrosio was accepted by Huskey and a short while later, I had my interview and joined them. Huskey now had his engineering staff. We were later joined by our junior engineer, Harry Larson, and programmer, Roselyn Siegel Lipkis. Those that made the drawings and put the SWAC together were:

Brent Alford, Draftsman
Arnold Dolmatz, Technician
Blanche Eidem, Assembler
Sidney Green, Draftsman
Harold Luxemberg, Technician
Michael Markakis, Technician
John Newberger, Draftsman
James Walsh, Machinist

All of us were going to build the first computer in the Western United States. What meant more for each of us was that this was going to be the first computer any of us had ever built.

THE COMPUTER ROOM

In 1948, when Huskey came to the INA, the campus of UCLA was expanding rapidly. The veterans of World War II were getting their degrees under the GI Bill of Rights. The scene was totally different from the windowless offices of Aerospace that I had tolerated for the past year or two. The handsome buildings were situated in a park like setting with lots of greenery and wide open spaces between them. There was the pleasant coastal climate of Westwood Village; the polluting smog had not yet arrived and my office window provided a nice view of the Santa Monica mountains. The INA occupied some "temporary" World War II buildings up on the north end of the campus. They were single story wooden buildings that had now been turned from housing military classrooms into offices and computer rooms.

Although Huskey's new electronic computer was only in his imagination, there was already plenty of computing going on at the Institute. It all was taking place in the "computer room." Today, when most of us associate computing with the personal computers on everyone's desk, we don't often think of large computers. These computers hide out in rooms in large corporations and universities, continuously doing millions of calculations every second, usually having large magnetic tape recorders for recording the results of their calculations. This is the computer room of the '90's and so it had been for the previous four decades ever since the first electronic computers.

But the computer room at INA didn't house a giant computer; it contained a roomful of small desks. On each desk was an electrically powered mechanical calculator operated by a skilled woman. Each woman had a work sheet with the numbers that she was to use in her calculation in the left-hand column. These numbers are what we now call, the input data or simply the "input", derived from computer engineers. Across the top of the other columns were listed the operations (multiply, divide, subtract and so on) that she was to do using her mechanical calculator. This list of operations or instructions were like today's computer program. The mechanical calculator, like the arithmetic unit of a modern computer, produced the results of each operation. The operator copied these results and wrote them in the appropriate columns of her work sheet. The results of some of the operations became the input data for the next operation. These partial results were written down and temporarily stored on paper for reinsertion into the calculator. As the operator obtained each partial result, she wrote it in the appropriate column and went on to the next column. The final column contained the desired results, the output data or simply the "output."

The operations going on in the old computer room were really the following five operations that are performed by all computers, electronic or human, large or small:

One: The input of numbers
Two: The arithmetic operations—add, subtract, multiply and divide
Three: The storage of numbers in memory (the work sheet)
Four: The output of results
Five: Control and sequencing of the calculations through a program

What a noise whirring gears, clanking keys and dials made with twenty or thirty machines working simultaneously at full tilt. Imagine the errors that may have taken place. Calculations had to be repeated to be sure that they were right. All results were hand copied from the dials on the calculators as there were no printers or automatic typewriters to print the answers. Later, before electronic computers superceded the old computer room, some calculators were modified to automatically print the results. The dials were provided with switches so that their readings were connected to an electric typewriter. The numbers were then automatically printed in columns as the calculation was performed and a complete and orderly listing of the results was produced without error.

Ancient civilizations used marks in sand or pebbles and twigs for reckoning problems. As societies became more complex, the need for better ways to calculate inspired the invention of the abacus over 5000 years ago. The great scientist, Blaise Pascal, is credited with constructing the first desk adding machine in 1642.

Pascal built his machine to help his father do the

books for his business, and it must therefore have been the first business machine 300 years before IBM. His calculator used a wheel or disk to represent each one of the decimal digits. Each wheel was engraved with the digits 0 through 9 around its periphery and you could read the number standing in the machine by reading the position of the wheels through a small window in the cover. This same idea is used in the odometer part of your car's speedometer to count and display the number of miles travelled. Like your odometer, Pascal's wheels were connected by a carry mechanism so that as each wheel turns past nine back to zero it produced a carry to the next higher digit to the left by turning that wheel ahead by one. Unlike your odometer, Pascal's calculator had another set of wheels, a set that you could turn to put in the numbers that you wanted to add. As these input wheels were turned, they would rotate the main wheels which would perform the arithmetic and indicate the answer.

Pascal's desk calculator and others that were invented later didn't really become popular until the industrial revolution allowed them to be made in large numbers so that everyone could afford them. Among the inventors of mechanical desk adding machines and calculators were those that formed their own companies. Although many have now either gone out of business or merged with other companies, many of the older generation may still remember their names: Burroughs, Marchant, Monroe and Friden. But even then they didn't have the wide acceptance the electronic calculators have today.

As a child in England in the late 1920's my mother took me with her to the bank. Banks in those days were unlike the ones we have now which display themselves as friendly places where you can get home and auto loans and save your money. They were then very imposing buildings with marble floors and columns, high ornate ceilings and tellers sitting behind bars. Their hushed, almost holy, atmosphere were designed to strike awe in the customers. On that visit I saw a sight that has stuck in my mind ever since, partly I suppose, because I was reminded of it by my work on computers. A man was standing before a high desk in the back of the bank reciting numbers at a sing-song rate very much like the auctioneer at a tobacco or cattle auction. I asked mother what he was doing and she astonished me by saying that he was adding up the bank's books. It's hard enough to believe that a person that was good in mental arithmetic could accurately add up ordinary numbers, but the man in England was adding up pounds, shillings and pence. With 12 pence to a shilling and 20 shillings to a pound it was a feat that few of us can do today with pencil and paper.

These "talking" computers must have been very common in the last century when the inventor of the truly automatic calculator, Charles Babbage, was working on his "Difference Engine." Babbage's work was supported by the British government in order to promote the production of navigational tables for their navy. Thus, the major incentive for a calculator in the early 1800's was the same one that, as we have already seen, got the Bureau of Standards into the Mathematical Tables Project in 1938. Later the need for data reduction for the Census Bureau resulted in the construction of the SWAC. Babbage demonstrated a working model of his first automatic calculator in 1822 which ran on the mathematical principle of differences (see Appendix 1). He therefore called it his "Difference Engine."

The principle of differences allowed the Difference

Engine to calculate the values of the squares, cubes and higher powers of the numbers without multiplying but simply adding. The great men of science, Isaac Newton and Leonhard Euler, discovered before Babbage that many important mathematical functions, including those of trigonometry and Kepler's laws of planetary motion, can be represented by the sums of squares, cubes and so on. These could then be calculated by repeated additions using the method of differences. Babbage realized that the additions could be mechanized using number wheels like Pascal's adding machine but in a much more complex arrangement. The method of differences is just a simple example of the "algorithms" that modern computer programmers use to make the computer solve our problems.

However, the Difference Engine, although a fine conception in itself, was not the major contribution that Babbage made to the ideas behind modern computers. Having conceived of the Difference Engine, he immediately got the idea for a much more universal calculator, his "Analytical Engine." This marvelous machine foreshadowed the computers of today. It was to have its operations programmed by holes punched in cards, its partial results stored in thousands of wheels, its arithmetic performed mechanically in what Babbage called his "mill" and its results printed automatically. Thus it contained the five essential functions of a modern computer and it also contained a feature which, as we shall see later, all modern computers require—the ability to call for a change in its program. For example, it might come to a place in its calculations where it needed the square root of a number, in which case it would automatically ring a bell to alert the operator. The operator would insert a new punched card containing the program for square root and start the Analytical Engine again. If the operator gave it the wrong program, Babbage planned to have the bell ring twice until the operator did the right thing. Many of us would feel at home with this ringing bell as we are getting used to being beeped by our own personal computer if we press the wrong key.

Babbage was never able to get his Analytical Engine built as it was much more complicated than the Difference Engine of which he had made only a small model. The intricate gears and wheels were required in the thousands and were beyond the hand-made methods of the early clock makers. Perhaps he was too eager to build his Analytical Engine and should have completed a small model of the Difference Engine. He could then have demonstrated that a calculator could indeed do useful work by calculating a few navigation tables for the government and found support for his project.

In 1991 the Science Museum in London constructed a working model of Babbage's Difference Engine for the 200th anniversary of his birth. It consists of 4000 individual parts and was made using modern manufacturing methods. The original drawings still exist and were redrawn to reflect the machining tolerances that could have been maintained in Babbage's day. Earlier, in 1906, Babbage's son supervised the construction of the Analytical Engine's "mill" and proved that it would work by having it multiply the number "pi" by itself out to 29 decimal places.

The first machines that could be called computers in the sense of the Analytical Engine had to await the invention of the automatic telephone switchboard with their electric relays. These relays were combined with modern counting wheels in a large machine built by IBM in the late 1930's. This famous machine, the Automatic Sequence Controlled Calculator (ASCC), was the brain child of Dr. Howard Aiken of Harvard University. When it was completed, IBM gave it to Harvard where it was renamed the Harvard Mark I. Aiken was familiar with Babbage's work and also with the punched card calculators manufactured by IBM. Aiken wanted a machine to solve nonlinear differential equations. These mathematical equations describe many physical processes but can only be solved by numerical calculations. The result was a collaboration between Aiken and IBM engineers to build a machine that was in part similar to the Analytical Engine. Arithmetic operations were performed by literally thousands of counting wheels mounted on common shafts. Each number in the machine, up to 23 digits long, was stored by 23 wheels. The complete machine stored 72 numbers giving a total of 1656 wheels in all. When calculating, these wheels were turned by friction from the shafts and all the shafts were turned together by an electric motor delivering as much as four horsepower.

Babbage would have been quite at home with the Automatic Sequence Controlled Calculator as he had planned to drive his Analytical Engine, not with an electric motor since they had not yet been invented, but by the available power source of his day, a steam engine!

COUNTING
& NUMBERS

Nowadays children in grade school are taught that there are other number systems, or ways of counting, than the decimal system which we all use. The decimal system arose from the use of our earliest calculator, the ten fingers on our hands. Of course, just because we have ten fingers doesn't mean that all societies invariably came up with the decimal system. Many early civilizations, including the Aztecs of the New World, counted by sixties. This sexagesimal system is still used by us to keep track of minutes and seconds. The early calculating machines used the decimal system while all the later vacuum tube and modern computers use the binary, or count by two, system.

No one bothered to point out to me at school or even in college that there existed these and other numbering systems. My introduction to electronic counters at Aerospace was the first time I was enlightened on this subject. If you weren't brought up on these concepts, your first reaction on hearing about it is probably like mine was: What do you mean? Another number system? A number is a number, how can there be a different kind?

Once upon a time, as my version of the story goes, a wizard visited the great and wealthy Maharajah and showed him the latest technological achievements of the sorcerer's art, a genie that would do your every bidding, or as we shall see, almost your every bidding. The Maharajah immediately wanted to possess the genie and demanded that the wizard name his price, which could of course, be very large because the Maharajah was the richest man in the world. But the clever wizard did not want to get involved in haggling over a price and risk offending the Maharajah so he said:

"Being a man of very modest desires, I will sell you, O Maharajah, the genie for just a few pennies a day. If you will give me one penny today, two pennies the next day, four the next, and continue each day to double my fee, you will have paid me completely for the genie before the thirtieth day."

On hearing this simple offer the Maharajah thought to himself:

"Why that means four pennies on the third day, eight on the next. Even on the seventh day I will only owe this poor unsuspecting wizard 64 pennies. It shouldn't be very hard to pay him for only thirty days. What a bargain!" So he immediately made the agreement with the wizard and got the genie that would do his every bidding.

Now all of you that might have heard this story before know that on the thirtieth day the Maharajah had to try to come up with over twenty million dollars and even the genie couldn't come up with that much money!

As the story was told we find the result surprising but we wouldn't be so surprised if the story were changed so that the wizard would have asked, as before, for one penny the first day but then changed his terms so that he demanded 10 the second, 100 the next and so on for only six days. He would then have received a million dollars on the sixth day as we all know how to count one, ten, hundred, thousand, ten thousand, hundred thousand, one million. The wizard story has a surprising answer because we don't ordinarily work with the binary, count by two, system of the wizard.

In any calculator or computer, whether it uses beads like the abacus, number wheels like Harvard's Mark I, electric relays, vacuum tubes, transistors or integrated circuits, it is important in a practical machine to use as few elements as possible to store the numbers. This is where the doubling or binary system pays off.

Each bead in an abacus or each tooth on a number wheel represents numbers by either being in a certain rest or initial position, which represents zero, or in another position where it stands for a numeral. If you use your fingers to count, you might start with all your fingers closed to your fist to represent zero and then extend each finger, one at a time, to count. In this way you can count up to ten on your two hands. However, if we want to make an analogy between your fingers and a calculator wheel, we must remember that ten is written in our decimal system as a one followed by a zero. This means that each wheel, like the ones in your car's odometer, need represent only the digits from zero to nine. So to make our finger analogy correct, you should label your first finger zero, your second finger one and so on up to nine for both hands. You then hold out one finger at a time as you count, and if you want to go past nine to ten, you could use your toes to indicate the tens, starting with zero tens, one ten and so on up to nine tens. By holding up one finger and one toe (a good trick!) you can represent all the numbers from zero to ninety-nine with your twenty digits.

Now, if you were to use the wizard's system, you start with all your fingers closed to represent zero and your first finger is labelled one and the next stands for two as in our decimal example. But here you don't label your next finger three but label it four and keep on doubling, like the Maharajah had to do, going to four, eight, sixteen and so on up your tenth finger which will stand for 512. If you continued on with your toes, labelling your first toe 1024 (twice 512) and keep on doubling you will find your last toe stands for the large number, 524,288. Now, the trick to this new system is that you can hold up as many fingers and toes as you please. In the decimal system you could only hold up one finger for units and one toe for tens. In this new binary system you can hold up, say, your fingers labelled four and sixteen to represent twenty, fingers one and four to get five and if you hold up all your fingers and all your toes and then add up all the labels you will find that you are now representing 1,048,575!

With the binary system we have gained what the wizard saw but the Maharajah didn't. With your twenty digits you could only count to 99 with the decimal system, but with the binary system you can count to over a million with the same twenty digits. The first vacuum tube computer, the ENIAC, used tubes in place of your fingers. The designers, Eckert and Mauchly, patterned their computer after the existing decimal mechanical calculators and made it to store 20 numbers of 10 digits each. As we have seen this would require ten fingers for each of the ten digits in each of the twenty numbers, a total of 2000 fingers, which in the ENIAC corresponded to 2000 tubes. Since each tube was the size of an ordinary lamp bulb, this took up a lot of space and used a lot of electrical power. Like today's computers, those that were designed after the ENIAC used the binary system and could store each of ENIAC's ten-digit decimal numbers using 32 tubes. The twenty ten-digit numbers could then be stored with only 640 tubes, saving about two-thirds of the tubes.

In the decimal system we used ten fingers or numerals for each digit, while in the binary system we have only two numerals for each digit, 0 and 1. These two binary states were represented by having one of your fingers closed for 0 or open for 1, so altogether you had 10 binary digits on your fingers alone. If you wanted to record on paper the positions of your fingers, you could use this binary number notation and write a string of zeroes and ones to represent the position of each finger. For example, you may have held your fingers in the pattern written as 1001010101. This is a ten digit binary number that represents 597 in our decimal system. Each binary digit is called a "bit," so your fingers can store 10 bits, your fingers and toes 20 bits, and the ENIAC's 2000 tubes could have stored 100 20-bit numbers if it had used the binary number system.

When George Stibitz, mathematician and early computer pioneer at the Bell Telephone Laboratories, designed his computer in 1938, he used another number system to save equipment, sort of half decimal and half binary, called the bi-quinary system. This number system is interesting as it was used in the abacus as long as 5000 years ago. If you recall the construction of an abacus, it consists of many vertical rods with beads that slide along them. Each rod represents a decimal digit and is divided into two parts, one part having five beads while the other part has one. (Some versions have five and two beads, but the extra bead is only used to remember carries.) The five beads represent zero through four and the single bead stands for five, so that by a combination of both you can count to nine. The single bead is binary, the five beads quinary, therefore the abacus uses the bi-quinary system using only six beads instead of 10 for each digit.

Although Stibitz's computer really worked in decimal like the abacus, it could do so with six instead of 10 relays for each digit. If the ENIAC had used this system, it would have taken 1200 tubes instead of the 2000 to store the same 20 numbers. The bi-quinary system has the advantage over the binary system in that it is easy to convert the numbers to decimal so the operator can read them. Today's personal computer can convert from decimal to binary and back to decimal so quickly that we don't even know that it is working with binary numbers.

When the first electric typewriters were invented for automatically sending telegrams and thereby doing away with the old telegrapher with his clicking telegraph key, a five bit binary number was used to represent the 26 letters of the alphabet and a few punctuation marks. As you can easily verify, five fingers or bits can represent altogether 32 numbers from 0 to 31. The five-bit binary numbers or codes for each letter in the telegram could be recorded as holes punched in a long paper tape, the holes representing binary "1," the absence of a hole binary "0." Each five-bit code was punched across the tape followed by the next five bit code. When more than 32 different characters needed to be typed such as when it was desired to print capital as well as small letters, one of the codes was made to alternately operate the shift-lock key and the shift-unlock key on the typewriter. Later, at the time the first electronic computers were built, the number of holes across the tape was expanded to six representing a six-bit number so that 64 characters could be coded without using the shift key.

These six-bit codes were in use for a long time and were even used on the first computer magnetic tapes using six recording tracks, one for each bit. But as computers came to be used more and more in business, more characters were required. If you count up all the symbols used in printing, including upper and lower case letters, the numeric digits, punctuation marks, special symbols like dollar signs and the mathematical signs like plus and minus, you will find that there are over 100 of them. So IBM, in the late fiftics, made an eight-bit code standard for all computers. Its 256 possible values could code for all the letters and symbols. They coined the word "byte" for the eight-bits, which seems to be a play on the words "bit" and "bite" as in "a bite full of bits".

The eight-bit code or byte is now universally used and is standardized by the U.S. government. All computer systems now use this "American Standard Code for Information Interchange" or ASCII which is pronounced "ass-key" by computer buffs. So now we all hear about bytes whenever computers are discussed. The computer salespeople talk not only about bytes but also kilobytes (thousands of bytes) and megabytes (millions of bytes). They tell you how many megabytes there are in your computer's memory, how many bytes in the numbers your computer processes in its arithmetic unit and even how many bytes per second it can read from your floppy disk.

Isn't it wonderful what that wizard got us mixed up with?

THE SYMPOSIUM

In a recent move I discovered a handsomely bound volume that was acquired during my days at the SWAC entitled, "Proceedings of a Symposium on Large-Scale Digital Computing Machinery, 7-10 January 1947." This symposium was one of the first of its kind in the world and the forerunner of the present National Computer Conferences. It was sponsored by the U.S. Navy and the Bureau of Ordnance and was given under the auspices of Harvard University's Computation Laboratory. The director of the laboratory was Howard Aiken, whom we met in a previous chapter as a co-developer of the Mark I computer.

Nowadays, when it is not uncommon for a computer conference to be attended by tens of thousands, it is interesting to read in the preface of the proceedings written by Aiken that they had expected "perhaps some sixty persons to attend." However, there was even then more interest in computers than they had thought and finally a total of 336 attended much to the surprise and overwork of the arrangements committee. Small as the attendance seems to us now, the attendants, like those in today's meetings were drawn from a wide spectrum of disciplines. In perusing the list of attendants you would have found not only mathematicians and electrical engineers, but also life insurance actuaries, aeronautical engineers, business statisticians, astronomers, optical engineers, meteorologists, physicists, chemists, economists and representatives of all branches of the Armed Services. It must have been clear to all that these new computing machines were going to have a broad impact on our society.

Also among the attendants were all those who were directing and working on computers, including J. Presper Eckert, William Mauchly and Herman Goldstine, those responsible for the first electronic tube computer, the ENIAC.

The second session of the symposium was entitled "Existing Calculating Machines," the first paper given by Richard H. Babbage, the grandson of Charles Babbage. He described the Analytical Engine and presented some of Babbage's original notes. Then followed papers on the machines of that day of which there were only four. These four digital computers were the only ones in January, 1947 that were operating in the whole world. They were:

One: The IBM Automatic Sequence Controlled Calculator (ASCC) presented to Harvard in 1944 and renamed the Mark I.

Two: The Electronic Numerical Integrator and Calculator (ENIAC) finished at the Moore School of the University of Pennsylvania in 1946.

Three: The Bell Telephone Laboratory Relay Computing System finished in 1940.

Four:	The Harvard Mark II Relay Calculator, Aiken's latest machine just being completed for demonstration at the Symposium.

These machines are listed in the accompanying chart, Table 1, along with Babbage's Analytical Engine and another early electronic computer constructed at Iowa State University but never completed. For each machine is shown the date it was first conceived and when it was finished, its storage or memory capacity with the total amount of numbers and digits in each number, a very brief summary of how it was programmed, and lastly, the major scientists and engineers who worked on the development and construction. The table also includes IBM's Selective Sequence Electronic Calculator (SSEC), which was the largest machine of its type ever constructed. Using both vacuum tubes and relays, it stored over 150 numbers which, as we shall see in Chapter 8, allowed it to be classified as a "stored program" machine.

The table also includes the Iowa State computer built in 1939 which was the unique creation of Dr. John Atanasoff. He is now credited with the design and construction of the first vacuum tube computer. It used a novel means for the storage of numbers, electrical capacitors. Capacitors hold an electric charge just as you do when you walk across a carpeted floor in dry weather. If you get charged up, a spark will fly off your finger when you touch a door knob and if you are not charged up then no spark. Atanasoff used 3200 small capacitors which could be charged or not charged to represent the 0s and 1s of binary numbers. His arithmetic unit used vacuum tubes which made it much faster than the other computers of the time that used either mechanical wheels or telephone relays. The machine was not really a general purpose computer as it was more like Babbage's Difference Engine than the Analytical Engine. Its control circuits were wired to do one and only one important task: the solution of simultaneous algebraic equations. Although parts of the machine were built and proven, it was never put into full-scale operation. Atanasoff didn't publish his work so it didn't make a contribution to the development of computers. In 1971 the ENIAC patent case was being litigated and the court decided that Atanasoff was the true inventor of the electronic computer because he had his idea so early. The patent that Eckert and Mauchly had on the first working electronic computer, the ENIAC, was therefore declared null and void. This ruling, of course, started up a controversy of who really invented the computer. This controversy can be resolved by giving everyone credit. Atanasoff gets the credit for the idea of a vacuum tube computer and Eckert and Mauchly get credit for going a big step further and making one that actually worked.

There was another computer development that started before World War II which took place not in the U.S., but across the Atlantic in Nazi Germany. The inventor, Konrad Zuse, was unknown to American computer pioneers. He built several small computers in his own home, first using telephone relays and later vacuum tubes. He realized that vacuum tubes would give his computer speed and reliability and he also, like Atanasoff, saw the value of using binary numbers. His machines were true general purpose calculators and he is given credit by some for the first operating computer using the stored program concept. His third and largest model, the Z3, used both tubes and relays and had a storage capacity for 64 numbers, each 22 bits long. He got little help from the German government as Hitler believed that he would win the war

TABLE 1
EARLY COMPUTERS IN THE UNITED STATES

TYPE	NAME	YEAR START	YEAR FINISH	MEMORY NUMBERS	WORD DIGITS	PROGRAM STORAGE AND CONTROL	BUILDER
Mechanical	Analytical Engine	1833	Never	1000	50	Jacquard Cards Rings Bell for the Operator	Charles Babbage Lady Ada Lovelace
Electro-Mechanical	Mark I or ASCC	1939	1944	72	23	Punched Tape Subsequence Unit Choice Register	H. Aiken, Harvard Durkee, Hamilton and Lake, IBM
Relay	Bell Labs Model V	1938	1940	15	7	5 Punched Tapes Discriminator	George Stibitz Bell Telephone
Relay	Mark II	1944	1947	100	10	4 Punched Tapes Branch on Sign	Howard Aiken Harvard University
Relay	SSEC	1945	1948	8 (Tubes)	19	38 Tape Loops Tape Punch & 10 Reading Stas.	Frank Hamilton John McPherson
				155 (Relays)	19	Instructions Like Data	IBM
Vacuum Tubes	Iowa State	1939	never	64 Binary	50 Bits	Hardwired for Algebraic Equations	John Atanasoff Iowa State College
Vacuum Tubes	ENIAC	1943	1946	20	10	Switches, Patch Cords, Preprogram-med Sequence of Subroutines. Later had stored program	J. P. Eckert and John Mauchly Moore School of Engineering University of Pennsylvania

in less than two years and Zuse's machine would be too late to help. As it was, the war took a different turn and allied bombers destroyed Zuse's apartment and the Z3. Zuse managed to escape to Switzerland with a small working model. After the war he worked for IBM and continued to design computers in Germany.

In all these computers the arithmetic operations were controlled by having the computer read punched cards, like the Analytical Engine, or punched tape, like the Z3, or by wiring up patch boards like the ENIAC. Every computer must have a method of control so that a program of operations can be properly executed. Even the women working in the computer room at INA needed a method to properly sequence their operations. Let's see how this was done.

DECISIONS 

In that old computer room at INA when one of the women in the course of her calculations came to a point where she needed to change the calculation procedure or calculate a new mathematical function, she would get another work sheet from the mathematician in charge. As we saw earlier, when Babbage's Analytical Engine needed to change programs it rang a bell to get help from the operator. But when George Stibitz's Bell Telephone Laboratories computer needed a new program it was able to switch control to any one of its five program tapes. It knew when to switch control because its arithmetic unit contained what Stibitz called a "discriminator."

A paper on the Bell Lab's machine was given at the 1947 Harvard Conference by Samuel Williams. In his paper he referred to his computer's program tapes as routine tapes according to the modern usage in which programs are made up of routines and subroutines. He compared manual computing with his relay computer and effectively summed up this relationship in the following paragraph:

> The operations performed by manual effort are replaced by automatic operations performed by relays. In manual computations the arithmetic operations are performed by persons making use of mechanical calculating machines, slide rules, tables or longhand calculations. In the automatic computing system, a relay calculator receives the numbers and the desired operational information electrically, performs the calculation in much the same manner as a mechanical calculator, and delivers the result electrically.

The numbers and operational information came from electrical switches that sensed holes in punched paper "input" tapes. The results were delivered to electric punches that punched holes in the "output" tape. Thus these tapes contained the input and output data of the automatic computer. Williams then discussed the operation of the program or routine tapes:

> An important attribute of a trained manual computer is his or her ability to make decisions as the solution of the problem progresses. This is done by examining and comparing the values of numbers. The relay computer is provided with a discriminator which, with the aid of the calculator, examines the numbers presented to it by the routine and signals the routine control to proceed with the same routine, substitute a different routine, or terminate

the computation, thus guiding the computation in
a fashion similar to that of a manual computer.

In this age of the computer it seems strange for us to call
a person a computer, but we must remember that the
manual computer just referred to by Williams is a person
who's computing, not an adding machine or pocket calculator.

When one of these manual computers was instructed to change routines when the results of a calculation was, for example, less than 100, he or she was trained
to recognize this fact and take appropriate action. In order to make the computer do this, the computer engineer
could use several methods. One that seems simple enough
at first sight would be to provide a mechanism that gave
an electrical signal when a value less than, say, 100 appeared in the computer's arithmetic unit. But this method
would have the limitation that it would only respond to
100, not to 101 or any other number that might be required in future problems. A general method of sensing
when a program change should be made is a device like
the discriminator of the Bell Lab's machine. The discriminator was made to sense whether the result was positive
or negative. How was this sign discriminator used when,
as in our example, the computer needed to sense when
the answer was 100?

The constant 100 was stored in one of the
calculator's relay number stores and at suitable intervals
during the computation the calculator was programmed
to subtract this from the result. If the subtraction yielded
a negative number, the result was less than 100 and if
positive, it was greater than 100. The discriminator sensed
the sign of the result and if the number came up negative,

the computer automatically branched to a new routine on another tape.

The Harvard University Mark II had four program or routine tapes and this "branch on sign" feature. This feature was so important that IBM's relay and tube computer, the SSEC (Selective Sequence Electronic Calculator) had 38 control tapes and could even punch out new control tapes which it could later automatically read back in. This computer was one of the first computers, if not the earliest, to have instructions represented in the same way as the input data. This was accomplished by giving the instructions the form of numeric codes that could be stored in the computer memory in the same way as numbers. The Bell Lab's machine used letters and numbers as well as algebraic signs on its routine tapes. For example, to add two numbers you would punch out a teletype tape that contained the message:

BH + CH = TEO

BH and CH told the machine it was numbers B and C that you wanted to add and TEO told the machine to hold the answer in its storage relays.

Although this method is simple enough for a programmer, it means that programs cannot be produced by the calculator itself since it can only punch out numbers, not letters and symbols. But in the SSEC the instruction letters and symbols were represented by some agreed upon number codes like 1 for add and 2 for subtract, and so on for multiply and divide. This is the system used in today's computers originally proposed by Eckert and Mauchly in 1944 when they were inventing the next generation of computers.

Byron Phelps in his 1980 article on early IBM computers quotes a brochure handed out at the 1948 demonstration of the SSEC which sums up the advantages of this concept:

> Because the instructions are set up in numerical form with no distinction between them and the numerical values of the problem, computed modifications of these instructions may be made as the calculation progresses.

Although the control system of the SSEC enabled the machine to modify its own program, the punched paper tape was far to slow for a high-speed vacuum tube computer. Even if the computer could calculate quickly, the instructions could not be read from the tape fast enough. So the first vacuum tube digital computer, the ENIAC, used an electronic sequencer to provide the instructions at electronic speeds. Programming was done by using switches and patch cords similar to those used in the old telephone switchboards. The unique control system was designed to solve the equations that described the motion of a projectile. The control unit, the "Master Programmer," selected different routines that were programmed using the patch cords. Each routine could be programmed to repeat the desired number of times. Like the Bell Laboratories Computer and the SSEC, the Master Programmer could be programmed to branch to a different routine based on the sign of a number. So the ENIAC worked like the relay machines but was much faster and its speed was not limited by the punched-paper tapes.

However, the positioning of all the ENIAC's switches and connecting all the patch cords to program a single problem took many hours. During this time the ENIAC could not be used for computing. But once it started computing, it was thousands of times faster than the earlier relay computers and could do many calculations in a hurry. So the bottleneck was the programming and later the ENIAC, too, was equipped to have its program coded as numbers and stored in electronic memory.

Although the SSEC could store instructions and numbers interchangeably in its relay memory and on paper tape, its storage was so limited that it really didn't have the flexibility of the modern computer with its high speed and high capacity memory. It wasn't until the organization of the modern computer was invented that the nature of a computer was changed. Rather than being a machine that just grinds out solutions to mathematical equations, it became a device that can make logical decisions. A device that now permeates the work place and our homes. This invention was made by the work of three people, a physicist, an engineer and a mathematician. These three are well known to all computer historians and we shall see as we recount their story that their ideas gave us the digital computer as we now know it. They were the ones that started the computer revolution.

THE STORED PROGRAM CONCEPT

One of the major incentives for automatic calculators was the need for mathematical tables. This held true for the development of vacuum tube computers as it also did for Charles Babbage. During World War II the mathematical tables that were in great demand were the firing and bombing tables for the guns of the Armed Services. These tables were published as pocket-size booklets so that the gunner could look up the angle to elevate his gun so he could hit his target. From the knowledge of the distance to the target, the prevailing winds, the temperature of the air and the type of shells he was using, he could look at the appropriate table in his book and train his gun accordingly. During the war automatic special purpose computers were developed to train the guns and the Air Force bombers had their automatic bomb sights. Yet these automatic machines had to be designed to work in accordance with the same rules as laid out in the gunner's firing tables. In fact, the numerical information of the tables were incorporated into these machines.

The Aberdeen Proving Ground in Maryland was the Army's major test facility for all types of artillery. Located at the proving ground was the Ballistics Research Laboratory (BRL) devoted to research on the flight and design of projectiles. It was also BRL's responsibility to produce firing tables for the Army's gunners. The laboratory was under war time pressure to provide these tables on a timely basis and wasn't able to keep up with the demand using the only available computers, the women and their mechanical calculators.

There existed a machine that could help BRL, the differential analyzer invented before the war by the famous electrical engineer Vannevar Bush at MIT. This was an analog, not a digital computer and it used gears, differentials and mechanical integrators. It could solve the mathematical equations describing the flight of projectiles and draw the results as graphs on a sheet of paper. The firing tables could then be read from these graphs. Close to BRL at the University of Pennsylvania, another differential analyzer had been built and was in operation at the Moore School of Engineering. The Moore School also had a computer room with women operating hand calculators. In 1941 BRL contracted with the Moore School to produce firing tables. Many more women were added to the computer room and the differential analyzer was kept busy. At this time John Mauchly came to the Moore School to take a summer course in electronics.

John Mauchly was born in Cincinnati, Ohio on August 30, 1907. His family later moved to Maryland and he attended Johns Hopkins University in Baltimore to study engineering and physics. He obtained his Doctorate in Physics in 1932. After graduating he became an instructor and later Professor of Physics at Ursinus College, a small school in Collegeville, Pennsylvania, near Philadelphia. He was encouraged to follow an academic career by his father who was Chairman of the Department of Terrestrial Magnetism at the Carnegie Institution in Washington, D.C. Mauchly's interest in numerical calculations began with his research work in meteorology and the prediction of weather. His calculations involved large amounts of data and he found, as we would expect, that human computers did not meet his needs, so in the late thirties he started to design machines that would do his calculations quicker. He first tried to adapt the existing punched-card tabulating machines and later he conceived of a completely new type of computer that would use vacuum tubes. In the summer of 1941, in order to learn more about electronics so he could further his ideas on computers, he went to an Engineering-Science-Management War Training (ESMWT) course at the Moore School. The purpose of this course, sponsored by the government, was to teach electronics to scientists so they could better contribute to practical war-related projects.

Hearing of the firing table work at Moore School, Mauchly told his idea for a vacuum tube computer to Professor John Grist Brainerd, the technical liaison man with BRL. Mauchly wrote a memo in 1942 entitled, "The Use of High Speed Vacuum Tube Devices for Calculating." Imagine the excitement this must have caused at BRL when they realized that this new computer would work thousands of times faster than the over-worked women and their calculators. In fact, it was predicted that the new computer could do in one day all the calculations that 25 women could do in three months.

One person who caught the excitement of this new idea was Herman H. Goldstine, a mathematician recently drafted into the Army and assigned as liaison officer between BRL and the Moore School. Goldstine quickly saw the possibilities for the electronic computer and it was in large part due to his efforts that a contract was given to the Moore School in April 1943 to design and construct the world's first general-purpose vacuum-tube digital computer, the ENIAC.

Mauchly was helped in the preparation of his proposal by a young research assistant at the Moore School, J. Presper Eckert, Jr. Eckert, a brilliant electrical engineer, was then working on electronic research projects for the war effort, destined to become the Chief Engineer of the ENIAC and later Mauchly's partner in the manufacture of computers. Eckert was born in Philadelphia in 1919 but unlike Mauchly, whose father was a theoretician, his father was a self-made man who got his education by mail order and night school. He had started a business on a shoe string and became a successful real estate developer and a one-time millionaire. Because of his father's interest in business, Eckert had entrepreneurial ideas which must have had a great influence on his later decision to go into business with Mauchly. However, in 1941 this was some years into the future and Eckert was a graduate student at the Moore School and was serving as a laboratory assistant at the class attended by Mauchly. When Mauchly discussed his computer ideas with Eckert, he immediately saw that they were feasible. He looked up all the literature on electronic counters and became a self-made expert that enabled him to contribute his electrical engineering knowledge to Mauchly's proposal.

By the summer of 1944 the ENIAC was well under

construction. The team of engineers under Eckert included Arthur W. Burks, Robert Shaw and T. Kite Sharpless. In April, Harry Huskey, who was an Instructor in the Department of Mathematics at the University, joined the Moore School of Electrical Engineering part time. His first tasks were to work on the IBM punched card equipment used for the input and output of data and to familiarize himself with the programming of the ENIAC. All these people went on to contribute to other computer projects after the ENIAC was finished. The project proceeded rapidly as they all worked with great enthusiasm on what they believed would be a breakthrough in the art of calculating. But the real breakthrough came during the course of the project when Eckert and Mauchly had time to consider what the next machine should be like. In their off hours, whenever they could get a moment away from the ENIAC, they had many discussions about the next generation of computers. In an article Mauchly wrote for *Datamation magazine*, he stated:

> But all through 1944, and in 1945 as well, we were leading a double life. For much of two shifts, from 8 A.M. to midnight, ENIAC construction and testing needed supervision. Then as hourly workers went home and project engineers thinned out, Eckert and I were left to consider the 'next machine.'

They realized the need for a larger store of numbers. Even relay computers had gradually increased their memory capacity. The Bell Lab's machine had the capacity to store 15 numbers while the later SSEC could store 155 numbers. But how could a large electronic memory be made when the ENIAC, even with 18,000 vacuum tubes, could store only 20 numbers?

Of course, as we have seen, a great saving in the number of tubes could be had if the new computer were to use the binary number system. The binary system would have saved about two-thirds of the tubes that ENIAC used for storage. Thus instead of 30 numbers, it would be possible to store about 100 numbers with the same amount of tubes. But Eckert and Mauchly realized that a computer must be able to store not just hundreds, but thousands of numbers. Even with the binary system, this large a memory used an impractical number of tubes. A new and novel approach was required.

Eckert had worked with the newly invented radars. Radars operate by repeatedly sending out pulses of radio waves and between pulses they listen for any reflections or radio wave "echoes" from nearby objects. The transmitted pulse travels at the speed of light so that the echoes arrive after a very short but electronically significant delay. Similarly, when you shout near a cliff and get an echo back, the delay is long enough for you to sense because sound travels much slower than radio waves. Electrical pulses travelling down a cable also travel near the speed of light and it takes a long cable to produce a significant delay. But these pulses can be delayed for a considerable time by converting them to pulses of sound and sending them through a tube filled with a liquid. The sound or acoustic pulses are produced at one end of the tube and when they reach the other end they are converted back to electrical pulses. A similar delay happens in a poorly installed public address system when the sound from the loud speakers are picked up by the microphone which converts them back to electrical signals that are again amplified and activate the loudspeakers. This "feedback" of the sound delayed through the air between speaker and microphone causes the familiar loud singing sound.

Radar engineers developed this sonic delay principle to delay the pulses received by a radar. The delay was produced by sending high-frequency ultra-sound pulses down a tube of mercury. The electric pulses were applied to a crystal transducer which acted like a loudspeaker and sent the ultra-sound pulse down the tube. At the other end a similar crystal acted as a microphone and sensed the ultra-sound pulses which were now delayed by the time taken for them to travel through the mercury. The delay was equivalent to sending an electrical pulse through a very long cable or telephone line, for this reason the mercury delay units were called "acoustic delay lines" or "mercury delay lines."

The radar engineers used the mercury delay lines to make a "moving target indicator." Each transmitted pulse from a radar is reflected from many objects far and near. The received signal is thus a "train" of pulses, those from nearby objects being received before those from far away objects. If the two received pulse trains from sequential transmitted pulses are not the same (and the radar antenna remains fixed), one or more of the objects must have moved in the interim between transmitted pulses. By using the mercury delay line, the first train of pulses could be delayed to occur at the same time as the second train. These two trains were then electronically compared, thereby eliminating all pulses except those that represent a moving object. The delay line therefore allowed the engineers to sense these moving objects such as enemy airplanes, and display them. Eckert knew of these moving target indicators and planned to use the mercury delay lines for storing binary numbers. His idea worked like this:

Suppose you wanted to remember a list of numbers but instead of remembering them in your head, you stood in a canyon where there was a good solid echo and you shouted the numbers in quick succession and waited to hear the echo. As you heard the numbers come back on the echo you would quickly repeat each one and send it back across the canyon. Thus travelling across the canyon and back are sound waves representing your numbers and they will remain "stored" in the echo as long as you keep repeating them.

Instead of the canyon Eckert used the mercury delay line and in place of the spoken numbers he used the ultra-sound pulses to represent the digits of a binary number, a pulse representing the two binary states by being either present or absent. The task of repeating the numbers was then taken over by a vacuum tube amplifier that took the pulses from the crystal "microphone" on the receiving end of the mercury tube, regenerated them, and sent them back to the crystal "speaker" at the transmitting end. The pulses would then continue to go round and round and Eckert calculated that as many as 1024 pulses could be sustained, all travelling at once, like a juggler with 1024 balls in the air. One mercury tube, only a few feet long, with the addition of only 10 vacuum tubes, could store the equivalent of about 300 decimal digits. If these were stored in the same manner as the ENIAC, it would have taken over 3000 vacuum tubes, each tube the size of an electric lamp bulb. His idea proved successful in 1948 when he built and operated the BINAC, the first computer to use a mercury delay line memory.

When Eckert and Mauchly dreamt of this much electronic memory, the idea came to them that mercury delay lines could also store the instructions as well as numbers.

As we saw in the last chapter, the SSEC had program tapes for the instructions while the ENIAC had the master sequencer for control. In both machines, the instruction memory was separate from the number memory. But rather than have two separate mercury delay line memories, one for instructions and one for numbers, Eckert and Mauchly had the idea to store the instructions and numbers in the same memory. In this way not only would the instructions be available to the computer at high speed, but the computer could then change, or even develop its own instructions at electronic speeds. It turns out that they had then invented the modern computer and the idea of putting the entire program of instructions in the memory along with the numbers is called the "Stored Program Concept."

Eckert recalled some years later this was his "best computer idea," but it quickly became accepted by the ENIAC staff as "an 'obvious idea,' and one that we started to take for granted." Huskey later recalled that when he arrived at the ENIAC project in 1944, he had immediately heard about storing programs in the same storage as computer data. He later told Eckert that "My immediate reaction was 'Why didn't I think of that?'"

That may have well had been the end of it and the breakthrough that had become obvious may not have been appreciated for what it was. The first report containing the idea was made in January 1944 and was immediately stamped "CONFIDENTIAL" and no one would see it again until many years after the war had ended. It was going to be left to a brilliant mathematician to fully appreciate this concept and tell it to the world.

LOOPS
WITHIN LOOPS

As we have seen, in the summer of 1944 the ENIAC was well under construction and Eckert and Mauchly were working around the clock. Then came one of those chance happenings that many times have a major effect on the course of history—this one having a great effect on the history of computers.

Goldstine, the liaison officer between the Moore School and BRL, was one of many that saw the possibilities of electronic computing and had pushed for the ENIAC project. Having been to BRL on business, he was returning to the Moore School in Philadelphia. He was waiting on the railroad platform in the small town of Aberdeen for his train to arrive. To his surprise he saw the famous mathematician, John von Neumann, also waiting on the platform for the train. He had immediately recognized von Neumann—although they had never met—but he had heard him lecture several times. As Goldstine tells of this meeting in his book on the history of computers, he worked up the courage to approach this famous person:

> It was therefore with considerable temerity that I approached this world famous figure, introduced myself, and started talking. Fortunately for me von Neumann was a warm, friendly person who did his best to make people feel relaxed in his presence. The conversation soon turned to my work. When it became clear to von Neumann that I was concerned with the development of an electronic computer capable of 333 multiplications per second, the whole atmosphere changed from one of relaxed good humor to one more like the oral examination for the doctor's degree in mathematics.

Goldstine had touched a subject dear to von Neumann's heart and found himself trying to answer all sorts of questions about the ENIAC. Although von Neumann had done theoretical work on self-governing machines and robots, this was the first time he had ever heard of an electronic computer. But it didn't take his brilliant mind very long to absorb all that Goldstine could tell him so he arranged to visit the project.

John von Neumann, born in Budapest, Hungary, came to the United States during the 1930's to avoid the political turmoil in Europe, as did many other brilliant scientists of that era. He was appointed Professor of Mathematics at the Institute for Advanced Study (IAS) in Princeton, New Jersey. Being on the staff of IAS was a high honor, "home" of the best known "brains" in the world, including Albert Einstein. Among other things, while he was at IAS he became deeply involved in the mathematical description of supersonic and turbulent flows in liquids and by the beginning of the war, he was a leading expert on shock waves. This expertise was one reason he was visiting BRL as a consultant to the Department of Ordnance. They were of course interested in his theory of the shock waves given off by supersonic rifle and artillery shells. He held many other important posts during the war and was a major contributor to the atomic bomb project at the Los Alamos National Laboratory in New Mexico. He was also on the Scientific Advisory Committee of BRL and had been attending a committee meeting when he happened to be at the railroad station and met Goldstine. With all these credentials he had earned a significant respect in the scientific community, which later enabled him to yield great influence on the development and architecture of digital computers. Von Neumann immediately saw that the ENIAC would make possible the solution of complicated physical problems associated with the design of nuclear weapons. Beyond that immediate need, he also foresaw the general application of computers to mathematical research on his new theory of automata or robots.

Starting in September, 1944, Von Neumann arranged to regularly visit with Eckert and Mauchly. They were flattered by the interest shown by this famous mathematician and they shared their ideas with him. They described their plans for the ENIAC successor, the EDVAC, which was to include the Stored Program Concept. The large memory, the storage of instructions in the same memory as the data and the speed of the machine were instantly absorbed by von Neumann's logical mind. These ideas had been put down in Eckert and Mauchly's report of January, 1944 and finally in their progress report on the EDVAC written in September, 1945. Discussions with von Neumann were recorded in short minutes of each meeting. Since the mere existence of the Moore School project was a defense "secret," all these reports were classified and they could not be disseminated outside of the project.

Of course von Neumann as a consultant to BRL had access to these reports and saw an analogy between the EDVAC design and the organization of neurons in the brain, which cause the way animals function. Much to the amusement of the engineers he referred to the different sections of a computer as "organs" and likened the computer circuits to be analogous to the workings of neurons. Modern research in physiology has shown that each neuron in the brain is many thousands of times more complicated than simple vacuum tube computer circuits. The number of neurons in the brain vastly exceeds the number of memory and logic elements even in today's largest computers. But von Neumann's over-simplified analogy was his way to see the engineers' concept in totality and translate the operation of their hardware in terms of logical mathematical organization. The particular hardware a computer is made of, be it tubes, transistors or simple neurons, has no theoretical effect on the power of the computer.

Although certain aspects of these ideas were described in the classified reports and memos, there was never a full report describing the development of the new computer concept in one integrated paper. This was partly because the ENIAC staff was so busy and partly because engineers have a distaste for paper work. This all changed with the arrival of von Neumann, whose mathematical background had trained him to write and publish papers on great ideas. Publishing papers was the way to spread information on the latest developments among the scientific community. This was where von Neumann's interest lay and he saw the great value of the electronic computer.

In June, 1945 after about eight months of visits to the ENIAC and considerable thought to computer organization, von Neumann wrote his famous paper, "The First Draft Report on the EDVAC," as a memo to the Moore School. He described the power of the Stored-Program Concept and outlined the logical design of the new stored program machine. He organized and expanded on Eckert's and Mauchly's ideas and again used analogies to living creatures, calling the parts of the computer "organs." He saw the great power that lay in the use of a large memory with instructions stored as numbers. He described the concept of the "variable address code" which allows the computer to change its own instructions.

Goldstine, the young mathematician, was impressed by the Draft Report. Having been written by von Neumann, who was not a direct employee of the ENIAC project, it did not fall under the military contract that required all documents to be classified. It was written as a memo to the Moore School itself and at Goldstine's initiative, it was immediately circulated among people inside and outside the Moore School. It subsequently ended up in the hands of many people far and wide. The report, probably carried by Hartree on his return to England, came into the possession of Wilkes at Cambridge University where he would later build the EDSAC. Since von Neumann signed only his name to the report and because of his prestige in the scientific community he was immediately credited with the invention of the Stored Program Concept. It is true that von Neumann never claimed that the ideas were only his, but it is also fair to say that it was an oversight on his part not to have mentioned Eckert and Mauchly. Over the years he never troubled to directly acknowledge their contribution. Perhaps he felt that all the fuss about who invented the computer was not relevant to the progress of science.

Eckert and Mauchly saw the computer as an important aid to government and industry and were convinced that the only way to start the computer revolution was through the commercial manufacture of computers. They felt that they were the inventors of the computer and were entitled to patents on their ideas. Eckert must have been largely influenced to go to into business for himself by his father the self-made businessman. On the other hand, von Neumann and Goldstine came from an academic background and saw the computer as an invaluable research tool in mathematics. They wanted the ideas to be shared with all the scientists of the world. In this way they thought the computer would make its best contribution to society. So here we have the old conflict between practical engineers and academic mathematicians. As it turned out they were both right and they all, in their own way, started the computer revolution.

Events at the Moore School started happening quickly between the summers of 1945 and 1946. A new man, Irven Travis, was appointed Supervisor of Research and he firmed up the school's policy on patents. His new policy required that engineers sign a patent agreement assigning all rights to the school. This is the policy now in effect in most industrial research and development organizations. The companies pay the engineers for their services and in turn receive the patents. Eckert and Mauchly wanted the patents for themselves and refused to sign the agreement and in April, soon after the dedication of the ENIAC, they decided to leave the Moore School to start their own computer company. It was then that Huskey was denied the offer to head up the ENIAC project, so he left the Moore School in June. Goldstine and Burks both accepted job offers from von Neumann to work on his computer at the Institute for Advanced Study (IAS) in Princeton.

All this, as you can imagine, produced hard feelings at the Moore School between Eckert and Mauchly on one hand, and von Neumann on the other. Each thought the other was trying to get full credit for the invention of the modern computer and Eckert and Mauchly were greatly disappointed about the patent situation. Even though this charged atmosphere existed, the university and others proposed that a joint venture be formed to proceed with the construction of the EDVAC. The proposed project would be carried out jointly with Moore School and von Neumann at the IAS. They welcomed other industrial and academic interests who might gain from contributing financially to the project. Although on the surface this seemed to be a good way to fund the project, the tension between the different parties was bound to make it a failure. To make matters worse, von Neumann was trying to get a computer project started of his own and discussed a design with the U. S. Weather Bureau and the electronic giant, the Radio Corporation of America (RCA). The press got wind of this meeting and it was reported in the *New York Times* that von Neumann and RCA were planning to embark on a machine to aid weather forecasting. Eckert, Mauchly and the Moore School were not mentioned. This was not entirely an oversight, as the project was still classified, but Eckert and Mauchly took it badly because the paper gave the impression that the von Neumann and RCA project was the only one in existence at the time.

Von Neumann continued his campaign to keep computers in the universities and convinced the IAS to break from their traditional role as a research center and approve the engineering and construction of a computer. This computer was based on a design worked out by von Neumann, Goldstine and Burks and became know as the IAS machine. The two mathematicians urgently needed engineers to build their machine. Rather than follow Eckert's lead and use the mercury delay line memory, they wanted a faster memory and contracted with RCA to build a special memory tube called the Selectron. Both Goldstine and Burks were offered and accepted jobs at the IAS in early 1946 and the project was underway.

At the same time von Neumann offered a job to Eckert. However, there seemed to be no doubt at this time that Eckert had bigger and potentially more lucrative plans than to work for a modest salary in a university environment. He was just planning his computer business with Mauchly, so he did not reply to von Neumann's job offer. This obviously piqued the great mathematician and he wrote a letter to Eckert in March, 1946 which is quoted by Nancy Stern in her paper "John von Neumann's Influence on Electronic Digital Computing, 1944-1946." In the letter von Neumann points out the conflict between Eckert's interest in the commercial aspects of automatic computing and the "requirements and the stability" of his project at the IAS. He further goes on to say that he could no longer delay the project or limit it in any way, which may have been possible if Eckert had accepted his offer. He ends by declaring "our offer made to you as null." Since it would seem that Eckert, by his failure to reply, had indicated his lack of interest in the offer, von Neumann's letter seems unnecessary, seeming to fire Eckert before he was hired. It further indicates the conflicting interests between engineers and mathematicians. Eckert's plans for a commercial computer business just weren't compatible with von Neumann's academic research project.

The final episode to this story took place two years later when Eckert and Mauchly attempted to file for a patent on their design for the stored program computer, the EDVAC. The EDVAC used Eckert's mercury delay lines for its memory and was later built at the Moore School. They failed to get a patent, not because they were not found to be the inventors, but on a technicality in patent law. The Patent Office has a rule that if you publish your idea more than a year before you file for a patent, the idea is public knowledge and unpatentable. Even though von Neumann's report was never published in a book or technical magazine, Goldstine had distributed it outside the laboratory and as we have seen, even sent it all the way to England where Wilkes was later to build his own computer, the EDSAC. So the Army's attorney advised the Moore School, Eckert and Mauchly that the distribution of the report was considered to be a "publication" in the legal sense, therefore they could not obtain a patent on the Stored Program Concept.

Who the real inventor of the modern computer was has been argued by computer people and historians ever since the idea arose. There has been a great amount of litigation on the matter without a patent being issued. The influence of John von Neumann has secured him the title of the inventor of the computer especially among those who live in great awe of his achievements in mathematics. Without him the concept would certainly not have had the impact on the development of computers that it did. But the lack of a patent didn't discourage Eckert and Mauchly from forming their own computing company, the Electronic

Control Company. They made a computer called the BINAC for Northrop Aircraft and then, as the Eckert and Mauchly Corporation, made the famous UNIVAC for the Census Bureau. They showed the practical side of the computer and its applications to everyday problems. Eckert and Mauchly Corporation was eventually bought out by Remington Rand which merged to form Sperry Rand. Together with IBM they showed that computers were indispensable to modern business and could be made and sold economically.

From our vantage point, fifty years after the ENIAC was completed, the fuss about the Stored Program Concept seems not to matter. In fact, the concept is usually not even mentioned in computer courses. As Eckert said, it has become an "obvious idea" and no one can think that a computer could be made in any other way. But without the idea there could not have been the computer revolution.

The importance of the Stored Program Concept can be better understood if we take a closer look at what the computer instruction does. First of all it tells the computer to do the desired arithmetic operation—add, subtract and so on. But the instruction also tells the computer where to look in its own memory to find those very numbers that it used in the arithmetic operation. The memory of the computer is numbered like post office boxes so that each number stored in memory is "addressed" or located by the number of its "post office box." The number in each address or "post office box" can not only be data for the arithmetic unit but can also, using the Stored Program Concept, be an instruction. The whole memory, although one single unit, can be thought of as being divided into two parts. One part consists of addresses that hold data and the other part consists of addresses that hold instructions that make up the software. The list of instructions representing a program is usually stored in sequential addresses and as the computer calculates, the control unit sequences through the addresses by adding "1" to the current address after each instruction is executed. The control follows this procedure until the program calls for a branch to skip to a new address where the next program or set of instructions begins. The new address is specified in the branch instruction. This can be a special instruction telling the computer that a branch must take place or it might be an instruction that operates like the "discriminator" in Stibitz's Bell Lab's computer. For example, if the result of a subtraction was negative, the control would get the next instruction from the new address specified in the subtract instruction. To perform a branch, the programmer inserts such an instruction in his program and the computer looks for the next instruction at the new address.

Thus the Stored Program computer can branch to different programs when the programmer requires it. But the program can do more than that, now that the instructions are stored like numbers. Like numbers they can be processed in the arithmetic section. Even other numbers can be added to the address in the instruction and thereby "modify" the original instruction. The number that modifies the instruction could either be one already stored in memory or one that was the result of a previous calculation. The modified instruction could well be part of a program that the computer later uses and when it performs this instruction, it will look at the new address for the next instruction. So we now can make the computer do a long series of calculations, following the instructions in our program, in which is buried a command to change another instruction in the same program. So as the computer keeps calculating, it keeps automatically changing its program to do different things. As Goldstine says in his book:

> This ability to modify the addresses of instructions is not merely aesthetically elegant, it is *absolutely* fundamental. (My emphasis)

As an example he states the problem of finding the square roots of many numbers stored in memory. If we couldn't modify an address, we would have to write a square root program for every number. These programs would differ only in the address that instructs the computer where in memory it should find the data number it should use in the square root program. With the ability to modify the address, we put an instruction in our program so that each time a square root is taken, the address of the number is changed and the computer automatically goes to the address of each number in sequence and evaluates the square root.

Not only is this just a labor saving device for the programmer, it means that the computer can operate in "loops." In Goldstine's example, first the computer calculates the square root of the first number, changes the address and loops back to the square root program to take the square root of the next number. After looping through the square root program enough times to do all the square roots, it can then be made to go on to the next program, putting the computer in a loop to do the next calculation. Just like some movies in which the writer uses a "flashback" to tell an earlier story and then uses another flashback within the original flashback, the computer can have loops within loops. Put hundreds of these program loops together and your computer now has the power to play games with you, do your accounting, ask you questions or even fly the space shuttle.

All this would not be possible without the Stored Program Concept. Without it computers would merely be fast calculators solving mathematical problems. Computers are computers because they use the Stored Program Concept.

So we have to admire von Neumann, Eckert and Mauchly for having such a tremendous idea even though they, and many historians since, have argued as to which of them were the real inventor. But it's always fun to think what might have been. What if Eckert and Mauchly would have gotten their patent? Think how great it would be to have a patent on each and every computer, from large main frames to personal computers, and receive a royalty on each and every one!

WHAT'S IN A NAME?

His mind is engaged in rapt contemplation
  Of the thought, of the thought, of the
  thought of his name:
      His ineffable effable
        Effanineaffable
Deep and inscrutable singular name.

T.S. Eliot, *The Naming of Cats*

All computers seem to need a name, or at least a few letters and a number. Our personal computers have names like Apple, Macintosh, Power PC or simply Personal Computer. The first computers also had names and it was the project leader's task to dream up a name for their computer.

Mauchly started the trend by naming the first computer the ENIAC. Most references tell us that this acronym stands for "Electronic Numerical Integrator and Automatic Calculator," but there seems to be a difference of opinion. At the 1947 Symposium on Large Scale Digital Calculating Machinery, what we now simply would call a computer symposium, Lewis Tabor presented a paper on the ENIAC which he said stands for "Electronic Numerical Integrator and Computer." The "and" crops up in the acronym as it does in RADAR, "Radio Detection AND Ranging."

The same thing happens with the name of the Moore Schools' stored program computer, the EDVAC. Mauchly, the co-inventor of the EDVAC should, if anyone, have known what EDVAC stood for. He said at the same 1947 Symposium that the initials stood for "Electronic Discrete Variable Arithmetic Computer." Yet later writers slipped in "Automatic" instead of "Arithmetic." No doubt this was a natural slip because later Eckert and Mauchly named their commercial computer the UNIVAC and the "A" really stood for "Automatic" as in "Universal Automatic Computer." They also named the BINAC, "Binary Automatic Computer."

With all the computers being named some acronym or another ending with "Automatic Computer," it was no wonder that the other computer projects followed suit. At first Huskey didn't want to follow the trend, if indeed in the early days you could call it a trend with only four or five existing computer projects. There of course were exceptions from the rule like the Whirlwind computer at MIT. Huskey knew the SWAC would be a fast computer, so he suggested the name "Zephyr." In fact, when *Newsweek* came out with an article on June 13, 1949, they used the headline "Talking Zephyr" and went on to talk about "the fabulous electronic brain machines [that] have been credited with power to predict the weather, compute salary payments, replace minor executives and produce synthetic 'emotions.'" It seems that they were more accurate in their predictions than they might have thought at the time. The article ends with a quotation from Huskey:

> Of course, the machine differs from man in that it is really only a slave that faithfully does just what you tell it to do. But, by locating where an airplane was an hour ago, it can predict where it will be an hour from now. That may be some sort of thinking. I don't care how deeply the Zephyr thinks, so long as it doesn't develop ambition and initiative.

There on the same page is a picture of Huskey and the caption is "Dr. Huskey: Slave Supervisor!"

But Zephyr, "a gentle wind from the west," didn't catch on. Some at the SEAC project in Washington good naturedly suggested that the name should be "Sirocco," "a hot wind from the desert." So the SWAC was, for a time, just called the Numerical Analysis Computer. But in early 1950, someone in the administration at NBS thought it would be a good thing if the computer being built in Washington and the one at the INA be named after the Bureau. So the eastern computer became the National Bureau of Standards Eastern Automatic Computer, the SEAC, and the western computer the National Bureau of Standards Western Automatic Computer, the SWAC. The full names were too long for anyone to use regularly, but the administration at NBS really wanted the Bureau's name to be associated with the computers. Therefore, when Huskey received the official memo naming the SWAC, he was instructed, when writing or speaking of the SWAC, that he first give the full unabbreviated name and then and only then could he refer to the computer as the SWAC.

So the SEAC and SWAC carried on the automatic computer tradition for computer names. But when von Neumann started his own project at IAS he didn't feel obliged to keep up with this "engineer's" way of naming things, so he never officially christened his computer, which was always referred to as the "IAS Machine." But in the early fifties the IAS machine had spawned many similar machines throughout the country and the names of many of these carried acronyms in the old style. These acronyms once caused a little confusion in books and articles on the history of computers.

One case in point was the second IAS machine built at the Los Alamos Scientific Laboratory from 1949 to 1952. This project was conceived as providing for the training of computer engineers which, as you might well imagine, were in short supply at the time. While von Neumann was first visiting the Moore School, N. Metropolis was working at Los Alamos and became involved in the programming of nuclear weapon problems on the ENIAC. After a short period as a faculty member at the University of Chicago, Metropolis returned to Los Alamos to direct the construction of this second IAS-type computer. In order to poke fun at all the other computer names ending in "AC" and in the attempt to discourage the naming of any more computers in that way, he jokingly suggested that the Los Alamos machine be dubbed the "MANIAC." But this suggestion had just the opposite effect that Metropolis had hoped for and before long MANIAC was the official name of the Los Alamos computer, much to his chagrin.

Unfortunately, sometime in the later years of computer history, the name became associated with MANIAC's parent, von Neumann's IAS machine. This error caused Metropolis to publish a correction in 1980 in the "Annals of the History of Computing." I don't believe anyone thought up any words for MANIAC to stand for but people continued to have fun with it. B. V. Bowden in his book "Faster Than Thought" suggested a second definition of "MANIAC" as "anyone who has been making or using digital computers for more than a few years." All of us who have had to struggle with an obstinate computer can relate to this definition.

Another mix up with names of IAS-type computers occurred with the name of the computer built at the RAND Corporation in Santa Monica. While the SWAC was being built, William Gunning of RAND spent considerable time at INA helping with the design of the Williams Tube memory. Being a major Air Force think tank, RAND was interested in keeping abreast with computer developments while Gunning was supposed to be merely an observer. However, he acted more as a consulting engineer and made a large contribution to the design of the SWAC. Later on he was joined at RAND by Willis Ware, who had worked with the IAS project. These two then built the machine at RAND.

Both Gunning and Ware knew von Neumann from their work and visits to the IAS project. Like everyone who knew him, they were impressed with John von Neumann's quick mind and powerful personality. Since they were building a machine based on the great man's ideas, they decided to honor him by naming their machine after him. In spite of von Neumann's objection to the "engineer's" naming practice, they decided on "John's Numerical Integrator and Calculator," coining the acronym "JOHNNIAC."

In some histories this name is found incorrectly spelled "JONIAC," or "JOHNIAC," but the correct spelling is with two N's.

The full list of acronyms is quite long and it's difficult to present it in its entirety. But some of the more famous ones, at least in the early fifties, were the ILLIAC at the University of Illinois, the RAYDAC of the Raytheon Corporation, the AVIDAC of the Argonne National Laboratories, the ORDVAC of the Ordnance Department, the SILLIAC of the University of Sidney in Australia and the follower of the SEAC, the DYSEAC. Most of these names incorporate the name of the institution in the acronym and I leave it to the reader to guess their decipherment.

It's possible that the UNIVAC, first built by Eckert and Mauchly and later by Sperry-Rand, was the last computer to have its name ending in "AC." IBM decided to number their electronic computers like the 701, 702 and 703, following on with the 360 series. Control Data did the same with their 6000 series. Now that we have the personal computer, it's nice to see real names come back in use again; but while it lasted, there were a lot of ACs.

TUBES GALORE 

The ENIAC had 18,000 vacuum tubes of the type used in the radios and radars of World War II. Each tube was as large as an ordinary light bulb and like the lamp, had a hot filament that glowed red when it was operating. An ordinary radio had five tubes and some expensive radios prided themselves on having as many as 21. Of course the pressures of the free marketplace meant that the radio engineers might have to incorporate a few dummy tubes in their design just to meet the competition. These dummy tubes had their filaments connected so they would glow red with the rest of the tubes and the proud owner could look into the back of his set and count 21 beautiful glowing glass "bottles." This sight is now forever lost today when thousands of transistors in the integrated circuits of pocket calculators are too small to be seen by the naked eye, even if they did glow. But imagine what a sight it would be if you could see them all sparkling as they flash on and off.

The SWAC, like other stored program computers, used the binary system and a special TV or "cathode ray" tube to store its numbers, so that it ended up with "only" about 2600 tubes or the equivalent of as many as 300 large radios—and there certainly were no dummies. No wonder the engineers had problems in designing all the interconnections between so many tubes and ensuring that they were all properly made. The interconnections were laid out in sketches, then copied to more formal schematic diagrams and then into lists of wiring tables to be given to the technicians for assembly. Much the same is still done today, but engineers now have the very computers we were creating to help them design the new ones.

The SWAC was the first computer "West of the Rockies." It also had two other firsts: It was both a parallel and synchronous machine. Let's see what this means.

There are many ways in which a computer can operate, irrespective of whether it's built out of tubes or transistors. Whichever way they work, they must produce the same result when adding two and two. Each of the early computer projects had a different design philosophy, or "architecture," for their computer. And each designer hoped that their design would prove to be optimum. There was one good way to find out, and that was to build them. It turned out that the SWAC computer was in many respects more like your personal computer than others, including its eastern counterpart, the SEAC.

The SEAC was the antithesis of the SWAC in that it computed in a serial manner. This serial type of computing was the result of the invention of the delay line storage and was also used by Eckert and Mauchly in the EDVAC, BINAC and UNIVAC. These computers operated on the digits of a number in sequence, that is serially, as they performed an addition, multiplication or other arithmetic operation. This is the way we do long addition in school, starting at the right and adding each digit and keeping track of the carries as we go along. A single adder circuit like the one designed by Eckert used 10 tubes and could add binary numbers of any length by operating serially on each digit. Adding a 37 bit number like those in the SWAC would take 37 operations.

Now the SWAC was a parallel rather than a serial machine and it was made to add all of its 37 digits at once with 37 adder circuits. Its arithmetic unit was therefore 37 times more complicated than the SEAC, but much faster. Von Neumann's IAS machine was also a parallel design, but unlike the SWAC, its designers took great pains to make it asynchronous. When we do long addition we don't go on adding the next two digits until we have completed adding the first two. We might be able to add one and one together quicker than we add nine and five, but we must allow whatever time it takes. Similarly, the IAS machine was designed so that each circuit had to complete its operation before the next one could start, so each circuit took its own time even if it became slower as the tubes wore out. But the SWAC, a synchronous machine, allotted a certain fixed time for each circuit to operate. If in designing the SWAC you allotted, one microsecond (a millionth of a second) to add two digits, then the adding circuits must perform the addition within one microsecond or an error would occur. It was good engineering practice to design the circuits to work up to twice as fast as necessary to insure a margin of safety as the tubes aged.

If you had put your hand on one of the high speed computing circuits in the SWAC, taking care not to get a shock as those old computers used hundreds of volts, the electrical capacity of your hand might slow down the circuit enough to cause an error. Not so in the asynchronous IAS machine. It would continue to run, waiting for the slow circuit to complete its operation and just operate more slowly but without error. I often had a chance to verify this effect when, in the early fifties, I was testing the JOHNNIAC computer which used the same IAS asynchronous design. Instead of my hand I used a large electrical capacitor, which had the effect of many hands, and the machine that was normally running millions of times per second would slow sufficiently so you could observe its operation every few seconds. If you completely disabled the circuit so that it could no longer perform its operation, the JOHNNIAC would stop and wait until the circuit was enabled. In this way, if a circuit failed you could look to see where the computer stopped in its calculations and find the fault. Perhaps it was in part due to this asynchronous feature that JOHNNIAC became one of the most reliable of the early computers.

Princeton's chief engineer for the IAS machine was Julian Bigelow, who had worked during the war at MIT with Norbert Weiner, the inventor of Cybernetics. Bigelow strongly felt that the asynchronous feature eliminated a possible source of error as components aged. He also thought that the machine would be free to operate just as fast as each circuit would allow. Each operation would start as soon as the previous one had finished and not wait for the next clock cycle. In the SWAC, even if a particular circuit happened to finish a little early, it would have to wait its allotted time until the next cycle began so that the basic rhythm or clock rate of the machine remained constant.

Today's personal computers are all designed on the

synchronous and parallel principle like the SWAC. The speed at which they operate depends mainly on the speed of the arithmetic unit or arithmetic logical unit (ALU), as it is now called. As higher speed computer chips are designed, the computer's internal clock can be made faster. So now your computer store salesperson talks about a 66 megacycle machine which has a clock that runs at 66 million cycles per second. Soon the speeds will no doubt increase and may soon reach or surpass 125 megacycles, 1000 times faster than the SWAC's clock.

The early stored program computers are listed in Table 2. They are arranged according to whether they used a serial or parallel design. The serial machines all used mercury delay line memories while the parallel machines used Williams or special tubes.

One problem that caused a great deal of concern among the early computer engineers, and one that made many people skeptical that they would ever work, was the usable life of the vacuum tubes. The average life of an ordinary radio tube was then about 3000 hours, some failing much sooner and some lasting over 10,000 hours. The ENIAC had 18,000 tubes and someone figured that if each one only lasted 3000 hours, you would have to replace a tube every 10 minutes on the average. But that was not the way it turned out. At first tubes with a short life would fail and be replaced. Then the short lived replacement tubes would fail and be replaced and so on. After a while only the long lived tubes remained and there could be extended periods of time without failures. By 1953, the SWAC had been complete for three years and the records showed that the average tube life was 8000 to 10,000 hours. Some computer projects weeded out the short lived tubes by operating them in a tester for a few hundred hours before putting them into the computer.

Even so, it still would be nice to know when a tube was becoming weak and about to fail so that a failure was less likely to come in the course of a long calculation, which would then have to be repeated. So the vacuum tube computers had methods to test them under extreme conditions of low or high voltages. A test program would be run to detect any error.

Everyone, including von Neumann, was concerned that a random error would occur in the calculation and go unnoticed, so a lot of work was done to equip computers with error checking circuits. A brute force error checking scheme was implemented in Eckert and Mauchly's BINAC, the machine made for Northrop Aircraft, delivered in 1948. It was the first operating stored program computer incorporating the EDVAC concept and Eckert's mercury delay line memory. Northrop wanted to see if it would be feasible to use a computer in the guidance system of an airplane. The BINAC had to be reliable and error-free. It was therefore built as two computers, each identical in operation and construction. They both operated at the same time and continuously checked each other's results. Today NASA calls this "complete redundancy error checking," and all of us who watched the first Space Shuttle flight on television kept hearing of the five computers aboard the Shuttle. Three out of four had to agree and the fifth was a spare, an elaboration of the scheme Eckert and Mauchly conceived 40 years before.

Not all of the concern with tube failures was unwarranted and in one case the failures were difficult to explain. As mentioned vacuum tubes have a hot filament or "cathode" that generates the electrons required for their operation. In normal use, like in old radios, the tubes were

TABLE 2
EARLY STORED PROGRAM COMPUTERS

TYPE	NAME	STORAGE WORDS	WORD BITS	YEAR STARTED	YEAR FINISHED	BUILDER
	EDVAC	1024	44	1945	1951	Moore School of Engineering Conceived by J. P. Eckert, John Mauchly, John von Neumann
SERIAL						
	EDSAC	1024	17	1947	1949	Cambridge University, England M. V. Wilkes, W. Renwick (Based on the EDVAC)
DELAY						
	BINAC	512	31	1947	1948	Computer Control Corporation J. P. Eckert, John Mauchly (Delivered to Northrop Aircraft)
LINE						
	UNIVAC	1000	12 (Decimal Digits)	1947	1951	Eckert-Mauchly Computer Corp. (Later Sperry-Rand Corp.) J. P. Eckert, John Mauchly (Delivered to the Census Bureau)
MEMORY						
	SEAC	512	44	1948	1950	National Bureau of Standards Samuel Alexander
	IAS	256[1]	40	1947	1952	Institute for Advanced Study Princeton University John von Neuman, Arthur Burks, Herman H. Goldstine
PARALLEL						
CRT	SWAC	256[2]	37	1948	1950	Institute for Numerical Analysis, National Bureau of Standards, UCLA, Los Angeles Harry D. Huskey
MEMORY	WHIRLWIND	256[3]	16	1947	1950	Massachusetts Institute of Technology, Jay Forrester

Notes: [1]Used Williams Tubes. Planned 1024 word Selectrons from RCA
[2]Used Williams Tubes. Planned 512 words
[3]Used Special MIT Tube. Planned 2048 words

always active and busily amplifying radio waves so the electrons kept flowing through them. But in a digital computer, the tubes were either on, with electrons flowing through them, or off without any electron flow. In the arithmetic unit the two states represented the binary number bits, 0 and 1, while in control units they are used to tell the computer to carry out this or that step in an instruction. In the course of computing, some steps were very infrequently performed and certain tubes remained turned off far longer than turned on. It was found that these tubes mysteriously failed sooner than the others even though the filament was still good.

It was like a fine watch that, if left on the shelf unwound for a long time, develops corrosion on its gears and refuses to run. Everyone had the mistaken common sense notion that those tubes that were resting would last longer than those that were in use. This was not the case and the failures were traced to certain chemical elements used in each tube's construction. When manufacturers took care to eliminate these elements from their production process, this "cathode poisoning" went away.

While the engineers were working on the SWAC, they heard a strange story from the engineers at the MIT Whirlwind project. Their computer was turned on and working properly when all of a sudden, there occurred an electrical arc between two terminal posts. This arc started a fire that destroyed a circuit containing many tubes. Here was another mysterious cause of failure. The circuit had been working for many hours before the failure occurred and many other similar circuits were working fine. The engineers examined the insulating material between similar pairs of terminals in other parts of the Whirlwind. Looking under a microscope they found that, although plenty of room had been left between terminals to withstand the voltage under normal conditions, some very fine metal "whiskers," thinner than a human hair, had gradually grown out from each terminal until they produced a short circuit. It turned out that these same kind of whiskers had been previously found by the Bell Telephone Laboratories. They had built the amplifiers for the undersea telephone cable across the Atlantic Ocean very carefully to expect as much as 20 years of reliable operation. They had long life tubes and the best quality construction, yet they failed like the Whirlwind computer from the slowly growing whiskers. Bell Labs found that the whiskers only grew when certain metals were used to coat the electric terminals and if these metals were avoided, everything would be all right. So the Whirlwind engineers were wiser and the SWAC engineers made sure that their computer wouldn't grow whiskers!

Fig. 1. The SWAC and Control Console.

The Williams Tube memory tubes are visible through the glass doors in the center. The control unit is on the left. The memory electronics (CRT Deflection amplifiers), the master clock and input-output electronics are on the right. The automatic electric typewriter, the primary means for manual data entry and for typing results, is just to the right of the console.

Above: **Fig. 2. Harry D. Huskey at the Control Console.**
The paper tape punch and reader for input and output of data
are on the left, the electric typewriter on the right.

Below: **Fig. 3. The Magnetic Drum and Card Reader/Punch.**
The drum and its electronics are in the cabinet, left rear. The
card reader/punch and its electronic cabinet are left of the
console. The paper tape equipment has been moved to the right.

Above: **Fig. 4. The Card Reader/Punches.**
The electronic cabinet on the left connects the near machine to the SWAC. Note the plug boards used to "program" these units.

Below: **Fig. 5. The Institute of Numerical Analysis (INA).**
The author stands near the building entrance. The SWAC room is immediately behind him. Note the "temporary" nature of this old World War II classroom.

Fig. 6. The SWAC Team at Work.

Huskey is overseeing the SWAC team at work on the control unit. From left to right are Harry Larson, Harry D. Huskey, a technician and the author. Some of the completed chassis are on the roll-around dolly in the foreground. The unfinished console is at the right rear. Two old Tektronix oscilloscopes are on the left.

Above: **Fig. 7. Harry D. Huskey Examines a Memory Chassis.**
Each of these large chassis stored only 256 bits. A small metal screen on the front of each unit allows the pattern of dots and dashes on the TV tube (CRT) to be seen.

The console panel contains from left to right: master power push-button switches with voltage monitor lamps above, three arrays of lamps that display the binary contents of the three arithmetic registers, memory monitor tubes (CRTs), lamps for the instruction register and various control functions and the far right, running time and voltage meters.

On the desk is a small control panel for the operator to start and stop the execution of the program and slowly step through each instruction.

Below: **Fig. 8. Williams Tube's Dots and Dashes.**
Although the final tubes stored 256 bits as dots and dashes, this picture shows how 512 bits may have been stored. The dashes, representing binary 1s, spell out "ZEPHYR," a name suggested early for the SWAC.

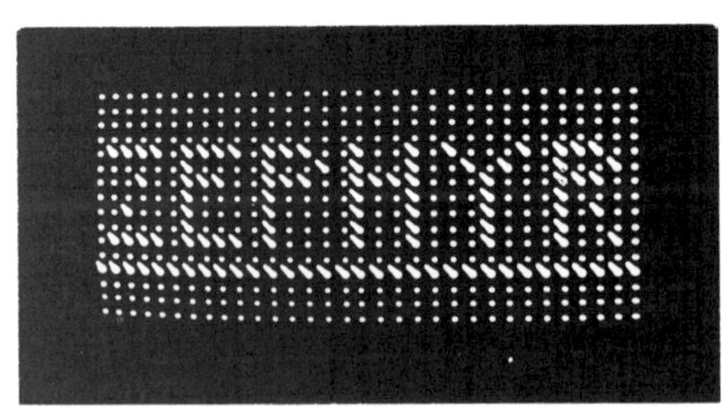

Left: **Fig 9. Ambrosio Checks the Wiring.**
He is standing between the two rows of electronic racks, the arithmetic unit and the memory and control units.

Right: **Fig. 10. The Memory Unit under Construction.**
The memory chassis have not yet been fitted with copper screens and front covers.

Left: **Fig. 11. An Arithmetic Unit Rack**

Three of these racks made up the full unit that occupied the back of the SWAC. The top row of chassis are plugged in. The second row will be installed in the connectors below them. The electrical delay lines hanging in loops were used to temporarily store the number when a "shift" command was executed.

Right: **Fig. 12. The Arithmetic Unit.**

The rack wiring is near completion. The far rack has a full complement of chassis while the two nearest ones are bare. The three plugs that held each chassis are clearly visible.

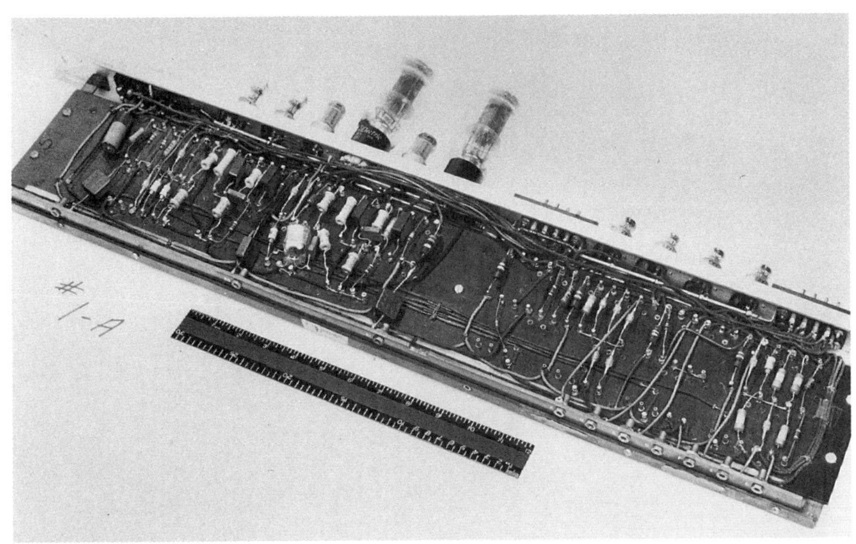

Fig. 13. The Two Arithmetic Unit Chassis.
There were a pair for each bit, 37 in all. The large tubes were used in the
high speed carry circuits. Each pair contains 22 tubes, a total of 814
tubes for 37 bits.

Fig. 14. The Memory and Control Racks.
These racks occupied the front of the SWAC. The wiring job has
only just begun. Some of the electrical delay lines are rolled up
and hanging in loops. Chassis await testing on the roll-around
dolly. The space for the memory chassis is visible behind the
control rack.

Fig. 15. The Control Unit being Tested.

The author is shown using a Tektronix oscilloscope. The vacuum-tube voltmeter on top was required to measure DC voltages which were not sensed by the old oscilloscopes.

Fig. 16. The Magnetic Drum.
The drum, about three feet long, was mounted with its axis vertical. Its shiny magnetic surface is visible behind the cables leading to the recording heads.

Left: **Fig. 17. SWAC Power Supply.**
A portion of the transformers and rectifiers used to supply DC power to the SWAC. The rectifier units were similar to those used in old battery chargers.

Right: **Fig. 18. A Power Distribution Panel.**
Lacey checks out the power control circuits. Above him are the fuses and sensors that turn off the SWAC if the voltages are not within limits.

GETTING STARTED 

We all admire the work of artists, musicians and fiction writers. Yet the works of scientists and engineers are sometimes thought of as being less imaginative and creative. This attitude creates an unhappy division in our society discouraging communication between the arts and science. Engineering is an applied science in that it builds on the understanding that science gives us on the way nature works. But scientists do more than discover the laws of nature. They create great insights through theories that combine the discoveries in one compact statement. Engineers and inventors use the discoveries of science to make practical devices that benefit us all. They don't merely take existing ideas and put them together in a routine way to create a machine any more than a painter merely puts existing blobs of paint on a canvas.

Human creativity takes many forms and our admiration should go out to all the disciplines of the arts, humanities, science and engineering. Each form makes its own contribution to human society. Every artist and engineer has a feeling of accomplishment in the work that he or she performs and this feeling is a vital part of his or her life. It's what makes life worth living to all of us when our work contributes, even in a small way, to the welfare and functioning of our society.

Engineering creativity is sometimes identified with invention and is given official recognition and encouragement by the Patent Office. We have seen how the invention of the computer did not result in any long lasting patents. Even the patent on the ENIAC was overturned in the early 1970's when a judge ruled that Atanasoff's computer was a prior invention. It was then too late for Atanasoff to apply for a patent himself. Yet the invention of the computer is one of the most important inventions of this century. Some even place it ahead of atomic energy, which fortunately has not given us nuclear war but has given us new medical techniques and a source of electric power. We have seen how Eckert and Mauchly lost a chance at their patent due to the Patent Office rules on prior publication. But creative acts can still be considered inventions even if they do not meet the requirements of the Patent Office. Throughout the history of technology there have been un-patentable inventions that had a large impact on society. These un-patentable inventions represent a real and important part of human creativity.

Another example of a great un-patentable invention is that of the early French automobile designer, Emile Levassor. He was the partner of Rene Panhard and their company, Panhard and Levassor, built cars until modern times. Before Levassor came along there were cars with gas engines, transmissions, differential gears, clutches, drive shafts and wheels. In fact all these things had been invented during the industrial revolution before any car was made. What Levassor did was to get the bright idea to put the engine in front, then the transmission behind it, followed by the drive shaft, differential and rear drive wheels. As any car buff or mechanic knows this successful arrangement was reproduced in every car up to the present time. Even your new front wheel drive car has the same arrangement compacted to drive the front wheels. Levassor and Panhard could not get a patent on their car because the French Patent Office said that any engineer skilled in the art could have made the same arrangement. But could any artist skilled in the art arrange blobs of paint to make the Mona Lisa?

Eckert, Mauchly and von Neumann may have had a patentable invention when they conceived the first stored program computer, but in many respects their invention was like Levassor and Panhard's. It could be said that they took existing calculating methods, combined them with the delay memories invented for radar, threw in some logical organization ideas and came up with the modern computer. But this would be belittling. For their achievement they should be as famous as Alexander Graham Bell or Thomas Alva Edison. But, like Levassor and Panhard, circumstances have given them relative anonymity.

But whether honored or not, they, like thousands of engineers working in less important projects, felt great excitement and true accomplishment when their ideas were built and proven in an operating machine. Here was something they created that had never existed before. This excitement is most keenly felt by those engineers that are fortunate enough to be able to take on projects single handedly or as parts of small teams. As projects become larger and require the labors and cooperation of many engineers, each one must sacrifice some of the individuality of his or her ideas to conform to the standards that insure that the final goal is met. I was fortunate to be part of the small team that Huskey put together to build the SWAC. We were about to feel the thrill of creating something important that never existed before.

Like Levassor and Panhard, we relied on electronic computer developments that either were already made or in the process of being developed in other computer projects. Huskey, unlike the rest of us and many other computer engineers at that time, had been able to acquire the knowledge of computer design from many different sources. He was first intimately associated with the ENIAC at Moore School and was one of the few to become first acquainted with the Stored Program Concept. He visited and evaluated all the English computer projects while he was in England. His year at NBS allowed him to observe the work of those at the MIT Whirlwind project, the start of von Neumann's computer at IAS and the initial design of the SEAC. Like Levassor, he put the techniques he had learnt all together and came up with the design for a different computer: a parallel, synchronous, stored program machine with a high-speed electronic memory that was to be the SWAC, the fastest computer in the world.

The arithmetic unit had to be designed to be fast. Huskey decided to use the fastest parallel adder then operating, the adder used by the Whirlwind computer. Sponsored by the Air Force, the Whirlwind was made to operate at high speed so it could be used in real-time operations for tracking friendly and enemy aircraft. It was the forerunner of the SAGE system that was the heart of the United States air defense system at the beginning of the

Cold War. It had to be fast and the Whirlwind engineers, under Jay Forrester, had taken great pains to make a fast arithmetic unit.

Huskey assigned Lacey to the task of modifying this design for the SWAC. The Whirlwind used only 16 bit numbers while the SWAC used 37 bits. For the arithmetic unit to have a similar speed the circuits would have to be made faster. So Lacey had to use faster circuits using vacuum tubes that required more power to operate. He made a mock-up of the new circuit to test its speed. He found that his new design allowed the SWAC to multiply two numbers in 296 microseconds while the original Whirlwind took 187 microseconds for only 16 bits and the serial SEAC took almost 3000 microseconds (see Appendix 2). With this fast arithmetic unit, Huskey was on his way to building the fastest computer in the world.

While Huskey was in England, he had visited the computer project at Manchester University under the direction of F. C. Williams. We have earlier noted that he was the inventor of the Williams Tube memory and a modified version of this memory is the one that NAML and Huskey decided to use for the SWAC. In early 1947, while Huskey was still in England, Williams had a working model of his memory that proved that it was a practical device. Many of the other computer projects were planning to use the delay line memories developed by Eckert for the EDVAC. Our rival at NBS, the SEAC, was also being constructed using a delay line memory. A third type of memory that was proposed by Engineering Research Associates used a magnetic drum. Magnetic drums were the forerunners of the hard disks we now have in our computers. They record the binary information as magnetic dots on the surface of the disk or drum, but they operate relatively slowly compared to electronic storage and are not suited to be the primary memory of a fast electronic computer.

Huskey assigned the development of the memory to Ambrosio. It was to prove the most difficult part of the SWAC requiring extensive development. Ambrosio was aided by Bill Gunning of RAND Corporation in Santa Monica and by Harry Larson, one of the SWAC's junior engineers. Williams used his tubes for a serial computer and they operated like a mercury delay line, each tube recirculating as many as 1024 bits. But the SWAC memory had to operate in parallel and instead of storing the bits in sequence, all 37 bits had to be stored at once. Thus in a very short time two numbers could be transferred from memory to the arithmetic unit, added together and the result stored back in memory. Let's see how the memory worked.

Imagine a portable television set, not one of those with a 19 inch or larger tube and yet not one of the pocket size that use a solid state screen. But imagine a television with a picture tube only 5 inches in diameter. On the screen of this tube you see a rectangular pattern of dots and dashes arranged 16 high and 16 wide. Each dash or dot lies within an imaginary square cell, like letters in a crossword puzzle, 256 cells altogether. The dots and dashes represent the binary digits, 0 and 1.

Now add more small TVs to your imaginary picture until you get a total of 37 and you are beginning to see the Williams Tube memory that Huskey imagined for the SWAC. The SWAC used 37 bit long numbers and the memory was designed to store 256 of these numbers. Huskey had hoped for 512 and even some optimists were suggesting 1024. These larger numbers would require double the number of cells on the TV screen (1024 requires 32 by 32 cells) which, as we shall see, was already too crowded. The first bit of all 256 SWAC numbers (or what we must call "words" as the numbers could also represent instructions) was stored on the first TV tube, the second bit of all the words on the second tube and so on for all 37 bits and 37 tubes. So by looking at a cell in the same place on the 37 TVs, you could see the dots and dashes and, if you were patient enough, write them down as strings of ones and zeros. This string of 37 bits represented one of the SWAC numbers in the memory.

So far in our imaginary picture we have assumed that the dots and dashes were coming from some TV station or VCR. If this were the case, the SWAC memory was really the TV station or VCR. There was of course no TV station or VCR inside the SWAC, so the TV tubes had to remember the pattern of dots and dashes all by themselves. This is where Williams' invention came to the rescue.

Williams noted that the dots and dashes produced not only a visible picture, but also an invisible electric charge pattern on the screen. So he placed a copper window screen on the front of the TV tube and connected it to a sensitive electronic amplifier. The electric pulses from the amplifier were different for a dot than for a dash. Williams used these pulses to control the TV signal so that it would continue to repeat the dots and dashes back to the screen and keep the stored pattern stable (see Appendix 3). In much the same manner as Eckert's delay line, the Williams Tube pattern was refreshed over and over. Instead of the bits being stored as sound pulses travelling down a tube of mercury, the Williams tube "pulses" were momentarily stored on the face of the TV tube.

In addition to the circuits that refreshed the Williams tube memory, there were also other circuits to allow the SWAC to select or "address" the 256 different cells. Then a dot or dash, representing 0 or 1, could be either produced ("written") or sensed ("read") as electric pulses that were sent to the arithmetic unit. The numbers and instructions that comprised the SWAC program were either typed in by hand on an electric typewriter or fed in automatically from punched paper tape. Once they were entered and stored in the memory, the SWAC was ready to run.

As we have seen, the SWAC was a synchronous machine. It was timed by an electronic "clock" that produced 125,000 electric pulses a second. These pulses were used to sequence the operations of the computer including the memory. A machine cycle was counted as the time between alternate clock pulses. When two numbers were to be added, they were each transferred to the arithmetic unit. This took two cycles, one for each number. At the end of the second cycle, the arithmetic unit would add the numbers and on the third memory cycle, the result would be written back into the proper address on the TV tubes' screens.

By the time I joined the project, both the preliminary design of the memory and arithmetic units were underway. You will remember that a computer has to perform the five functions: input, arithmetic, memory, output and control. Ambrosio was responsible for the memory and Lacey for the arithmetic. So by default, I inherited the responsibility for the remaining three, the control and input-output units. So Huskey started me on the most complicated of the three, the control unit.

The control unit had to sequence the operations of the memory and the arithmetic units so that the computer's instructions were obeyed. Each computer design uses a different set of instructions which are designated by a set of codes. Mainly this is done in an attempt to provide each new computer with a more flexible, faster and mathematically more powerful way of calculating. And the SWAC control was no exception. The parallel synchronous operation required it to have a different type of control than any of its contemporaries, making it a unique machine. Since another SWAC was never built, it was a one and only unique machine.

Huskey first had to decide how many instructions there should be. Of course there must be add, subtract and multiply, but there are many different ways that these operations can be performed and different methods to make the computer branch to different subroutincs. There are also logical operations and the ability to input or output numbers to punched paper tape or the keyboard and printer. Huskey wished to keep the number of instructions to a minimum and yet allow the SWAC to efficiently solve problems. This he was able to do with only 13 different instructions (see Appendix 4).

Before beginning the design of the control unit, I asked Huskey whether he had any specific way in which it should be designed and he said that he did not and I would have to use my imagination. So the task seemed overwhelming. I had to produce a control unit—using whatever means I could dream up that would interpret the list of instructions that Huskey gave me—one that would sequence the SWAC through each detailed step, unlike anything that had existed before. There I was, only two years from getting my Master's degree in electrical engineering, not having a single computer course, having learnt what a binary number was last year, told yesterday what a digital computer was and suddenly ordered to design a unique control section for a large general-purpose automatic computer.

Like an author commissioned to write a book, I decided to do some research. But was there anything to research? Computers were so new I was afraid that I would really have to start with only a pencil and blank sheet of paper. Some engineers would have gone ahead anyway without seeing how the same or similar problems were solved before. But if I tried that approach, I would later be haunted by the thought that someone had already done the same thing and I would have spent a lot of time reinventing the wheel so to speak. I immediately asked Huskey if he had any reports or books on computers and my request really paid off.

At first sight one might have thought that very little prior literature would have existed. Remember how the engineers at the Moore School wrote few reports on their computer designs and waited for von Neumann to write his First Draft Report. So I was happily surprised when Huskey handed me a large volume that the Moore School engineers had filled with descriptions of every type of circuit that could possibly be useful in the design of an electronic computer. All the special circuits with names like flip-flop, gate, adder, multiplier and so on, were listed. It was a true encyclopedia of computing circuits. Huskey himself was responsible for many of these reports. In 1946, he had assembled a five volume "Report on the Eniac," which served as a maintenance and service manual. After reading the Moore School report, I felt I had no need for further research, and it was a good thing, too because Huskey wanted the SWAC operating within a year and I had yet to put a mark on paper.

Because so many of the circuits were new, I had to design prototype units and evaluate their performance for inclusion in the control. We all knew that the circuits had to be designed to operate under the worst conditions that we could expect. The electrical characteristics of each electronic component could vary from the manufacturer's nominal value. They, along with the vacuum tubes, could change with age. Many years later, Julian Bigelow, Chief Engineer of the IAS project, recounts his trouble with circuits that required repeated readjustment. He had to impress on his engineers a standard set of circuit designs and procedures. These insured that, although one circuit may have worked properly, all similar circuits would also work, no matter how many were employed. Computer engineers in those days had to learn to design conservatively as their machines used circuits that, unlike those in radios and radar sets, had to be repeated hundreds of times.

For every design requirement there are many specific designs that may be used to accomplish the same purpose. If this were not true, we wouldn't have the many types of cars, bridges and buildings that delight us in their variety and at the same time, in their sameness. The engineer's job is to choose the most efficient design, and to do so, a comparison of alternate design should be made. The comparison may take the form of a mental picture of the different possibilities, but I have found it better if one makes a table enumerating each design approach with its pros and cons. From this table, the engineer makes a choice. It's a most important decision because once committed, it fixes the design of the machine. However, once the choice has been made, an engineer is usually able to later put forward all sorts of good reasons to justify that decision over and above the facts in the original table. In reality, the choice is seldom determined just by the facts and more often than not, the final decision is intuitive.

Intuition is the creative process that we highly admire in all the arts and sciences, even though we don't understand it. It's a decision or problem solving process that goes on in our brains and is influenced by all the knowledge that we have accumulated throughout our lives. Someday we may be able to better understand how our brains work and make these choices. It's a mystery how some people are better at it than others. Some studies have shown that experienced engineers solve problems better than those just out of school. So whether it's an engineer who decides on a good combination of circuits for a computer or whether it's a composer deciding on a good combination of musical notes, the results can be beautiful. I was fortunate to decide on a design for the SWAC control unit that eventually performed well and to me, that was beautiful.

WHILE WE WORKED

In a paper on the SWAC published in a 1950 issue of "Mathematical Tables and Other Aids to Computing," Huskey puts the project's starting date as January, 1949. He then says that by December, the SWAC was 80 percent complete. That year the engineering team all worked very hard, Huskey putting the finishes touches to the SWAC's overall specification and the engineers turning these into construction drawings for the technicians. The SWAC and the engineers' offices occupied a wing of the INA building by themselves and the engineers didn't often venture outside their domain. But while the engineers and Huskey were busy with the SWAC, a lot of work was going on in the other part of the INA.

This other part was the main reason for the existence of the Institute. Here's where the mathematicians had their offices. They came from all over the world to spend a few days, weeks, months and even years. The atmosphere was conducive to creative thinking. There were few nicer places than a sunny California campus where they could find a chance for casual interchange of ideas with colleagues. The main purpose of the mathematical research was what INA's name implies, numerical analysis. Mathematicians use many ways in which to analyze and solve mathematical problems. They have developed formulas for finding the solutions to many problems in algebra and calculus. Yet the work of the great mathematicians over the centuries have been stymied in their search for a formula, or analytical solution, to all the important problems. Those that they have not yet been able to solve sometimes yield to analysis by numerical calculation when theoretical analysis doesn't yield a neat solution.

An analytical solution to a problem provides a formula that gives a method of calculating the answer from the input data. Like Einstein's famous formula for the conversion of matter to energy, $E = Mc^2$, we only need to put in values for the mass, M, and the velocity of light, c, and immediately calculate the energy, E. Einstein worked long and hard to produce this formula from the equations that describe his theory of relativity. There are theories, like those describing the motion of fluids, that won't yield such simple answers. In these cases the mathematician can get numerical answers for particular values of the input data, but it requires a large amount of calculation. How this calculation is to be performed and whether it will yield answers of sufficient accuracy is the realm of numerical analysis. This important branch of mathematics yields solutions to practical scientific and engineering problems that could not be solved in any other way. Numerical analysis was given a great impetus when the electronic computer showed it was possible to do a great many more calculations in a reasonable time than what had ever been done before. The establishment of the INA was a result of this renewed interest.

Hartree of the University of Cambridge was acting chief when the INA started operations in the summer of 1948. The staff included John Todd from the University of London and Otto Szasz from the University of Cincinnati. These experts in mathematics were among many who were invited to the INA and found it a pleasant and intellectually stimulating place to do their research. They were also provided the means to prove their theories using the women calculators in the computer room, an IBM Card-Programmed Computer and later on, the SWAC.

When the INA was formed, a veteran of the Mathematical Tables Project, Gertrude Blanch, transferred from Washington. Blanch had been the scientific leader and manager of the people computing on their mechanical calculators at MTP. She finished up some tables that were left unfinished and in February, published a table of Bessel functions that are found in higher mathematical analysis. She then devoted her time to helping solve problems for the government and industrial establishments in the West. The aircraft industry and universities had problems that could only be solved by numerical calculation and Blanch kept the computer room busy. She went on to work with Roselyn Siegel on preparing problems for the SWAC. Siegel was later a common figure at the SWAC control console.

In late June, two symposia were held on subjects "pertinent to the effective utilization of automatic digital computing machinery." Huskey took time off from the SWAC to give a paper on "The Definition of an Automatic Digital Computing Machine" and also a paper on the solution of algebraic equations. Siegel gave a paper on the "Description of a Specific Automatic Computer." Of course both papers described the SWAC, which had yet to be given a name. These papers were followed by a practice session in which participants worked out "detailed routines" for the computer. In modern words they were studying how to program the SWAC. It seems awkward to us to refer to a computer as an "automatic digital calculating machine," but the use of the word "computer" for a human operator was still hanging on.

One highly regarded mathematician who joined the INA that year was Dr. Cornelius Lanczos. He, like von Neumann, was another one of the many brilliant people that emigrated from Hungary. In 1929 he worked with Einstein on his theory of relativity. He came to the U. S. in 1931 when he joined the staff of Purdue University. During World War II he worked on the Mathematical Tables Project for NBS. There he designed numerical analysis methods for the WPA workers using their mechanical desk calculators. These methods later turned out to be very suitable for electronic computers. He remained at INA until it was closed in 1953. He had written a textbook, Variation Principles of Mechanics, on the application of numerical analysis to problems in the mechanics of large groups of particles. Among other numerical analysis problems, he worked on the problem of inverting matrices, large groups of numbers that are used in advanced mathematics.

In September, Huskey took all the SWAC engineers with him on a trip to attend the "Symposium on Large-Scale Digital Calculating Machinery" at Harvard University. It was on this trip that we visited the SEAC and as we shall see in the next chapter, came home with new ideas from the SEAC project.

In October, Huskey was again giving a course on digital computers with the emphasis on the use of the SWAC. The announcement says that it was for the purpose of acquainting interested persons with the possibilities and limitations of high-speed digital computers. The course was attended by scientists from Western universities and industrial research laboratories as well as the staff of INA.

These classes and seminars were only a small part of the education work that the staff did over the five years of INA's existence. Computing is a field that crosses technical disciplines in the fields of mathematics, electrical engineering and physics. Most of those that were solving problems by numerical calculation belonged to one of these disciplines and each one had to cross over into the other fields without help, to learn the methods of numerical analysis. There were then no courses in computers or numerical analysis at universities like UCLA. So the INA cooperated with UCLA and gave courses to graduate students. These courses promoted the digital computer and started computing on the way to the professional status it has today.

The NBS also provided the means to promulgate information on computers throughout the engineering and scientific communities. It helped form the first professional computer society, the Association for Computing Machinery (ACM). John Curtiss, the head of NAML, was the first president, and later on Huskey held the same position.

It has been said that the commitment Curtiss brought to high-speed digital computers and the ability to attract scientists from throughout the country and Western Europe stimulated the construction and application of scientific computers. The INA wasn't just responsible for the fastest computer in the world but also for creating an intellectual climate where it would be accepted. A.S. Householder of the Oak Ridge National Laboratory says in his reminiscences, "To begin with numerical analysis *was* INA. One could hardly exaggerate its impact ... " It was at INA that numerical analysts and computer scientists crossed roads and laid the ground work for the computer revolution to come.

MAKING
IT WORK

In May, 1949, the SWAC was well under construction and I was still testing circuits that I chose from the Moore School report. Each one had to pass the worst state condition test and if the tests showed that I had made an error in my design calculations, I would have to go back and change the design. Meanwhile Lacey was busy making the detailed plans for the arithmetic unit. Each of the 37 bits were identical and it took 22 tubes for each bit. These tubes were mounted on two long thin chassis, each about three feet long, 12 tubes on one chassis and 10 on the other. These two chassis would plug one above the other into the electronic racks. The whole 37 bits of the arithmetic unit used 74 chassis and occupied the entire back part of the SWAC from one side to the other, a full 12 feet in length. Each chassis plugged into receptacles on the racks. There were three plugs per chassis and they were very robust so they could hold the weight of the chassis themselves. The plugs supplied the needed operating voltages and interconnection between bits, what engineers now call the "backplane."

September rolled around and I had yet to finalize my control design. Then Huskey took all three of us on a trip east to attend the second "Symposium on Large-Scale Digital Calculating Machinery" at Harvard. It was held to commemorate the dedication of Aiken's third computer, the Mark III. This one used magnetic drums for all storage instead of the relays in Mark II. It was a fast trip as in one week we visited the SEAC in Washington, the Whirlwind at MIT and the Symposium at Harvard. The exchange of ideas between us and the engineers in these groups helped in our own designs.

Henry Tropp commented on the exchange of ideas between computer projects in his paper on the Smithsonian Computer History Project, "The Effervescent Years: A Retrospective" in the IEEE Spectrum. He remarks how this communication between rival projects was unusual. Wilkes of Cambridge also found this open environment in the courses he was invited to in 1946 at the Moore School and in the many symposia he attended. Aiken's symposia, like the one we were attending, helped everyone to compare notes. But these open exchanges were not always the rule. As Bigelow says in his paper "Computer Development at the I. A. S. Princeton:"

Several people have asked questions about what we were thinking at the time, when we got our ideas, and in particular how much we knew about—and possibly gained from—developments taking place at other places such as project WHIRLWIND at MIT and the ex-Moore School team in Philadelphia. The answer is that we had no communication contact except rumors, and as far as I know each of these groups proceeded along its own avenues, directed its own goals and developed its own criteria of what constituted excellence.

In his own way, Bigelow was right. The IAS machine project relied heavily on von Neumann and input from other national laboratories. These other national laboratories were Los Alamos, Oak Ridge, Lawrence at Berkeley, Argonne in Illinois and RAND in California. They were all planning to reproduce the IAS computer at their facilities and were therefore interested in making suggestions as to how the machine should be built. It seems that we were kept ignorant of what was going on at Princeton. But we had a good interchange of ideas with the Harvard and Whirlwind projects and of course with the engineers at NBS who were designing the SEAC in Washington. This interchange gave me the last key piece for my design of the SWAC control unit.

The SEAC was a serial machine and used mercury delay lines for storage. In addition it used some extra electrical delay lines to store or delay short strings of pulses. Their chief engineer, Sam Alexander, made use of a delay line that was developed for radar use and was commercially available. It was a specially constructed co-axial cable and the thought struck me that I could use it to delay pulses in the control unit so they would appear at the proper times to sequence the operations of the SWAC. The SEAC group had put a lot of work into the design of a vacuum tube circuit to send pulses down the delay cable. This circuit used a special component called a "pulse transformer" that they built for themselves. These transformers were little coils about the size of one's thumb and used a band of a special ribbon made out of a magnetic material called "mu-metal." I learnt the specifications for constructing these transformers and soon had the SWAC technicians winding many of these little units. With my "discovery" of the pulse transformers, I was ready to get down to the task of drawing the detailed diagrams of the control unit. These diagrams showed how each control pulse was generated. These pulses would sequence the operations exactly according to the rules of arithmetic that were carefully laid out by Huskey. Any errors in the drawings and two plus two would not equal four or something just as disastrous might occur that was not so obvious.

The delay cables were used to produce properly timed pulses that made the arithmetic unit go through the detailed steps for each of the SWAC instructions. For example, if two steps were required, one following soon after the other, the control would send one pulse to the arithmetic unit to do the first step and at the same time, send this pulse through a short length of delay cable. When the pulse came out of the cable it was timed correctly to be sent to another part of the arithmetic unit to do the next step. A great many of these small steps were involved in the performance of the instructions and they were timed in this way by cascading different lengths of cable. These cables saved many tubes and had the additional advantage that they didn't wear out.

A good example of what the control had to do is shown by considering the steps involved in the execution of one of the simplest instructions, the addition of two numbers. The instruction took four cycles of the SWAC clock or 64 microseconds. It had four addresses: one specified where to find the first number, the second where to find the second number, the third where to put the sum and the fourth where to find the next instruction. In the first cycle, the control sent out pulses that were timed to reset the arithmetic unit to zero and send the first address to the memory control. Then further pulses transferred the contents of that address, the first number, from the memory tubes to the arithmetic unit. The control then sent a pulse to sense if the first number was negative and if it was, sent another pulse to the arithmetic unit to complement the number. (The complemented number when added will in effect be subtracted.) Thus six pulses were required for the first cycle, each one properly delayed so that the memory and arithmetic operated properly.

In the second cycle, the six pulses were again required to transfer the second number to the arithmetic unit. Then two additional pulses caused the computer to add the numbers and if the answer was negative, to complement the answer. The third cycle was relatively simple, using two pulses, one to transfer the address of the sum to the memory control and another to write the sum into memory. Finally, two more pulses were required to put the address of the next instruction into the memory control and read that instruction to the control. The control was now ready to perform the next instruction.

Altogether the control had to issue 18 pulses just to add two numbers. More complicated instructions took more steps and therefore more pulses. With all these pulses to generate, it took over 50 cables, ranging from one to eight feet long, to time them correctly. The cables were all wound up in loops and hung on the back of the control unit rack.

The SWAC was built before printed circuit boards

became available to ease the task of wiring. Every tube plugged into a socket with seven or eight connections. The 2600 tubes had over 20,000 connections on their sockets alone and each had to be wired by hand. And the wiring job was compounded further by the fact that each of the wires or components that were attached to the sockets had a similar number of connections on the other end. And then there were the 3700 crystal diodes which were very temperature sensitive. Great care had to be used when soldering them so that the heat wouldn't damage them. On top of all this there were large cables, each containing many hundreds of wires that ran up and down and between each rack to interconnect the chassis. The small team of skilled technicians and women assemblers had their hands full for a solid year wiring up the SWAC.

The most important tool that engineers had to check high speed circuits in those early days was the oscilloscope, made by the Tektronix company in Portland, Oregon. Every engineer today is familiar with the Tektronix name as they are still a leader in the manufacture of electronic test equipment. Few realize that they got their start right after World War II building a brand new kind of oscilloscope. Mention an oscilloscope to anyone not into electronics and you usually get a blank stare. But we are all now familiar with the heart monitors in hospital emergency rooms. These show a line of "blips" moving across a small TV-like screen which monitor the patient's heart beat. The blips are a moving graph of the electrical signals in the muscles of the patient's heart, like a graph of the stock market or daily temperatures. When the oscilloscope is used to check a computer, it shows the engineer a graph of the electrical pulses in the circuits. The engineer can then assess the correct operation by observing such things as how often they repeat, when they arrive with respect to other pulses and the shape of the pulses.

Oscilloscopes were invented in the early thirties and today they provide the basis for the screens of our TVs and the video screens of our personal computers. The TV picture tube and the oscilloscope tube are examples of cathode ray tubes or CRT's. The tubes come in very many different types, shapes and sizes. The SWAC memory tubes were standard tubes made for oscilloscopes. The heart of the CRT is the electron beam or "cathode ray" that writes the picture or graph on the screen in the front of the CRT. The cathode rays were discovered by the great scientist, Joseph Thomson, in 1897. The discovery of these electron rays started the whole world of electronics as we know it now.

During the war the oscilloscope was developed for observation of the fast pulses used in radars, and the success of Tektronix was in great part due to their being first to produce a commercial and more flexible version of the radar units. The pulses in the SWAC were for those days, very fast and short, lasting as little as one tenth of a millionth of a second. Only the Tektronix oscilloscopes were able to display such short pulses, so they were indispensable in checking the computer's "heart beats." During the summer of 1950, the SWAC was nearing completion and the pressure was on to get the control unit working. So I spent most of my waking hours looking intently at oscilloscope blips, so intently for so long that I would still see them dancing before my eyes as I went to sleep.

While I was having my hands full with the control, Huskey and Ambrosio were busy with the memory. At first sight the Williams tube seems easy enough to build. Just get a TV tube, a copper screen, an electronic amplifier and some electronic control circuits and off you go. But in practice there were many problems. As we have seen, Ambrosio was aided by Bill Gunning of the RAND Corporation. The memory is an important part of any computer and in those days was the hardest to design. Gunning and Huskey spent as much time as they could spare working with Ambrosio on the Williams tubes. Huskey said later that his struggles with the Williams tubes left him little time to think about much else.

Each of the 37 tubes were going to work together and if they got one working, then all they would have to do is build 36 more. So they first started work on a unit using a small three inch diameter tube. The first problem started when they turned on the amplifier that detected the small signals from the copper screen on the face of the tube. They found that the copper screen was acting like an antenna and instead of the proper signals appearing at its output, there was nothing but interfering radio signals. Huskey says in his paper on the SWAC that "all the radio stations would appear on the output full blast!" So a special metal box had to be built to enclose each of the tubes to shield against the interfering radio signals. These boxes had a metal screen in front so that one could observe the dots and dashes on the tube's face.

The three inch tube didn't really provide enough room between cells for reliable operation, so the next experimental unit used the final tubes with five inch diameter screens. The CRT's were standard off the shelf tubes as were many of the components that were used in the SWAC. Both the budget and time restraints prevented any thought of purchasing special tubes. These tubes were not manufactured to the exacting requirements of a computer memory and it really was not surprising that tests revealed small flaws in the phosphor coating on the back of the screen. These flaws produced interfering signals from the copper screen and caused certain cells to be unusable. Sometimes all 256 cells could be made to work if the circuits were adjusted to provide a rectangular rather than a square pattern. The flaws could then be made to lie between cells. It was going to be difficult to adjust all 37 tubes individually for best operation, but there was no choice but to go ahead and make the best of the situation. So a test program was established to select usable tubes from bad. Later in the early 1950s when IBM produced their first general purpose computer, the Model 701, they used Williams tubes in much the same manner as the SWAC. However, they were able to have their tubes specially made for them with the minimum of flaws. They then were able to obtain what Huskey had originally planned—512 cells on a three inch tube. These tubes were so reliable that IBM could use four tubes for each bit, giving their machine a memory capacity of 2048 words, eight times that of the SWAC.

The manufacturer of the tubes was contacted to see if the cause of the flaws could be ascertained. After some investigation it was found that the tubes were being built in a factory that previously had been used as a mattress factory. Very small pieces of lint still remaining from the mattress covers had contaminated the phosphor, giving the SWAC engineers an unwanted problem and very nearly preventing the SWAC from having any memory at all.

During the course of the memory design, F.C. Williams was able to visit the INA and provide valuable advice. But he was applying the tube for a serial rather than a parallel machine, so Ambrosio and his co-workers were very much on their own.

These and other technical problems were finally conquered and 37 units were built. They occupied a prominent place centered in the front of the SWAC stacked up five wide by eight high, leaving room for three more bits that might be possible in the future. They were mounted in a rack seven feet high by two feet deep and five feet wide. Altogether, it then took over a 100 cubic feet to house a memory storing 37 by 256 bits, less than 10,000 bits. Today 100 times or more can be stored on a microchip the size of your thumbnail. But it was then an achievement to have produced the first working memory for a computer that processed numbers in parallel just like your own personal computer.

The memory occupied a space in the center of the front row of racks just a few feet in front of the arithmetic unit. On each side of it sat two racks. The right hand rack housed the auxiliary memory circuits, the master clock and input-output units. The left hand rack contained the control unit. The two rows of racks, front row with memory and control and the back row with the arithmetic unit, were aligned close together so the wires that carried the 37 bits of information from the memory to the arithmetic unit would be as short as possible. The overall depth of the SWAC was a little over four feet, so it occupied about 50 square feet of floor space. This did not include the power supplies that were located on a wall outside the building.

After the schematic drawings were drawn, like Lacey and Ambrosio, I had to transfer the information to diagrams that showed the wiring of each of the many hundred tubes. The SWAC technicians could then assemble the chassis and give them back to the engineers for testing. The three engineers and the rest of the team were kept busy all during the last months of 1949 and throughout the first eight months of 1950. The first year was up in January and we were racing to see if we could get the SWAC working before the SEAC. So all of us were working 12 hours or more a day, making corrections in the chassis due to design and construction errors. Every wire had to be in the right place and every circuit had to work as planned before we could even think of trying to test the entire SWAC.

Then came the day when we could try all five units of the SWAC together and try adding two plus two. With larger numbers in special combinations, the arithmetic unit produced errors. We all helped Lacey look into the problem. You will remember that Lacey used a high power tube in each bit of the adder to get the required addition speed. This tube drew a lot of current and under certain conditions, all these tubes in all 37 adders switched on and off simultaneously. If this switching continued, it would produce such high current surges (up to 50 amperes) that the power supply couldn't handle it. So there was a big rush to obtain a larger supply so the arithmetic unit could perform correctly.

The SWAC then could be made to work reliably for short periods of time and even though there was still much work to be done, it was time to have the official dedication.

THE DEDICATION

In all the early computer projects it was very difficult even for experienced engineers to predict the time that would be required to complete their design and construction. Only the ENIAC engineers at the Moore School had the experience of seeing an electronic computer through to completion. But even they did not have any experience on a stored program computer with its entirely new configuration and experimental electronic memory. The new machines incorporated so many new ideas that there was little chance that anyone could have foreseen all the problems and have made a realistic schedule. Everyone was optimistic and tended to underestimate the tasks involved. This was partly because engineers usually oversimplify the magnitude of their projects and partly because the project leaders had to show their sponsors who had supplied the dollars, that the project would shortly be finished. Like the well publicized delays in the NASA space programs, things would inevitably go wrong and unexpected problems would show up. We have seen how the SWAC engineers had their share of problems with tubes and other components. These had been originally designed for radios, so care had to be taken to be sure that they would work in computer circuits. Sometimes, like the memory CRTs, they were operated in ways that their designers never imagined. Toward the end of 1949, the projected dates of completion came and passed so often that von Neumann came up with the law: A computer will be completed six months after the day on which you happened to ask.

But a day had to arrive when the computer was pronounced completed and a dedication ceremony scheduled. Usually it required that it run a program for a short time for example, a minimum of half an hour without error. When this task seemed to be in reach, a day was set for the dedication. For the many months that the SWAC was being assembled and tested, it consisted of two rows of open racks with plug-in chassis and tubes bristling along their sides. But it had to look finished before the dedication and more practically, it had to be enclosed so that cool air could be blown through it.

Huskey had originally counted on the cool West Los Angeles air, but later had to put in air conditioning. The SWAC consumed about 30,000 watts of electrical power and the air conditioner had to move 4800 cubic feet of air per minute through the cabinet to keep it cool. Unlike commercial computer companies like IBM, the project had neither the resources nor the facilities to make a metal cabinet 12 feet long, four feet wide and eight feet high, so Huskey enlisted the services of a sheet metal fabricator. All the plug-in chassis had to be accessible for servicing, so the cabinet had to have doors along its two sides. It was decided that the doors should be made of glass so that the electronic chassis inside would be visible. The least expensive glass doors were those made for shower baths, so shower bath doors it was. Many made fun of these doors saying that the fire sprinklers were not well placed for taking a shower.

But the glass doors, with their bright metal trim, made the SWAC take on a pleasing and impressive appearance. The center doors in front of the Williams tube memory allowed one to watch the little TV screens with lots of bright dots when the SWAC was running. The visible chassis gave the visitor an idea of the complication of making a machine with thousands of tubes. The name "NBS WESTERN AUTOMATIC COMPUTER" was written above the memory in bright metal letters.

In front of the SWAC was the control console, a standard steel desk with a sloping control panel on top. The panel contained the master power switches and voltmeters to monitor the power supplies. In the center were two CRTs of the same type as those used in the Williams tubes. You will remember that the memory tubes had 256 spots on the face in 16 columns and 16 rows. Each of the 256 locations was the address of a computer word. The two tubes on the console were also made to display on a 16 by 16 square. One tube merely put a dot on the screen at whatever address was being read or written to by the machine. When the SWAC was running, this spot would trace out lines on the screen as different addresses were accessed under control of the program. From this display the programmer could get some idea as to whether the program was using the instructions and data in the desired region of the memory.

The other tube could be switched to show the content of any one of the 37 memory tubes. On the actual tubes the storage of 1s and 0s was shown by dots and dashes, but on the console tube these dots and dashes were changed by a special circuit to short vertical lines for 1s and circles for 0s. (Today, our video terminals have circuits that display all the letters and numbers, but just generating a 1 and a 0 was novel in 1950.) So the programmer could stop the SWAC at any time and check the contents of the memory. Of course it would have been too time consuming to read all the 1s and 0s in this way, but a check of certain critical bits would serve as a clue as to the proper operation of the program.

On each side of the two monitor tubes there were neon lamps that indicated the contents of the registers in the arithmetic and control units. These were useful for detailed checking of the arithmetic unit's operation. The monitor CRTs and the neon lamps put on a good display for visitors.

When our eastern rival—the SEAC—was dedicated in June, Huskey decided that no time should be lost before the SWAC was dedicated. He checked his calendar and set the date for August 17. It was to be a grand affair and invitations were sent to all the important people in NBS and other computer projects. The dedication ceremonies were to be followed on the next day by a symposium on "The Application of Digital Computing Machinery to Scientific Problems." The problems they had in mind were those that were of interest to the aircraft companies and western universities.

Everyone worked day and night to get the SWAC in shape for the dedication. Not only did we have to get everything wired right and tested, but it had to operate without failure when the demonstration was required. It was a wonder that it did perform as well as it did. It actually took a few more years to find all the problems and make the SWAC a reliable computer suitable for daily use.

Dedication day began with the usual speeches. The Director of NBS, Edward Condon, came out from Washington to be the first speaker. He was followed by Air Force Colonel F. S. Seiler, Chief of the Office of Air Research, a large contributor of funds for the SWAC, who had flown out from Wright Field. Then came Dr. L. N. Ridenour, Dean of the Graduate School of the University of Illinois, and finally, the Chief of NAML, John Curtiss. Lastly our leader, Harry Huskey, now officially Chief of the INA Machine Development Unit, described the SWAC and gave a short demonstration. Everyone held their breath, but the hours of work had paid off and the SWAC did run.

All the newspaper people were there and the next day we were all amused by the articles in the paper about the new "electronic brain." The *Los Angeles Examiner* opened their article with:

> Prominent mathematicians attended the debut here yesterday of the world's fastest electronic computing machine and were not at all disturbed by the fact that it requires about four minutes to add 2 and 2.
>
> For, they discovered that in one extra minute the gleaming robot, with a "strong" mind and cooperative backbone, can perform nearly 1,000,000 more operations in addition.

They went on to add that the problem of 2 plus 2 was almost entirely devoted to programming the problem and entering on tape. The programmers must have been much amused at being requested to demonstrate such a simple problem. But it might well have been the first one that many of us would have thought of when confronted with the "gleaming robot."

Huskey is quoted as saying, "Naturally we'd never bore the machine with such an easy task," seeming to imply that the SWAC had emotions. Of course everyone wanted to know if it could think and the papers thought it best to try to calm the public. They said that the SWAC's creators aren't in the least in awe of it or fearful that it will replace the human brain. So it seems that the concerns many people had about the computer date back at least as far as the day when we celebrated the SWAC's dedication.

The next day the symposium gave a glimpse of what sort of problems were being planned to run on the SWAC. First there were the problems in pure and applied mathematics, including statistics and number theory. Then there were a host of papers on solutions to engineering problems. Scientists and mathematicians gave papers on topics such as the flight of an airplane when it starts a turn, nuclear reactor physics, perturbations of a rocket satellite, rocket engine research and a problem in astronomy. The computer was going to help solve all these problems. It was hard to imagine then that a computer would not only solve scientific problems, but would eventually help everyone in their home and office.

Some months after the dedication, the SWAC was running well enough for a problem to be run for hours without error. The mathematicians at INA, like mathematicians throughout the world, were interested in prime numbers. Numbers like 3, 5, 7, 11, 13 and so on that cannot be divided exactly by any number but themselves. As the numbers get bigger the primes keep getting further and further apart and are more difficult to find. Each number must be tested to see if a smaller number will divide into it exactly. Mathematicians who deal with the theory of numbers are very interested in finding large ones, so they programmed the SWAC to start with a known large prime and find a larger one. It was set to this task and after hours of calculating, it came up with a prime number larger than any yet known. This was an achievement only of real interest to mathematicians. But to all of us that had built a computer from "scratch" in less than 18 months, it was like a milestone in the history of computers.

POINTS
OF VIEW

Sometime during the construction of the SWAC Huskey was invited to appear on Groucho Marx's television show, "You Bet Your Life." The guests in the show formed teams that tried to answer a chosen list of questions correctly and win a prize. Before they chose their category of questions, Groucho interviewed them and was able to get a few laughs. When Huskey came on stage he was accompanied by a man who dealt in surplus materials. After Groucho had ascertained what they each did for a living, he asked Huskey how much the SWAC cost. Huskey replied "Over a 100,000 dollars." Groucho said "That much, eh?" and turned to the surplus dealer to ask him how much he would give Huskey for his fancy electronic brain. The "junk" man didn't have to think very long before he turned to Huskey and asked "How much does it weigh?"

Now from the junk man's point of view, the weight

of the computer might be its most precious asset and those old computers sure had it all over your lap-top computer in this respect. So far we have discussed the importance of the computer circuits, whether they are parallel or serial and how fast they work. We now call all that the "hardware" and from the point of view of a computer circuit designer, that may be the computer's most precious asset. But the most precious asset of a computer from everyone who uses one is the program or "software" that can do their job. The software enables people who don't understand the inner workings of the computer to directly apply it to their application. No computer manufacturer could sell one today without a complete package of software. And as much time is spent and money made in developing new software as in the design of new hardware. Yet in all the descriptions of the first computers, I haven't until now used the word "software." Was there software in those days and what was it like?

In 1950, the word "software" had not yet been coined and all computer programs were called "codes." We saw earlier how instructions that tell the computer what to do were originally punched into paper tape or cards. At first, special codes were used to stand for the desired operation, like + for add and - for subtract. Later the Stored Program Concept changed these codes to numbers so that the instructions could be stored in the computer's memory along with the data. It is these numeric orders that modern computers understand and when they are strung together to make a program, it makes sense to the machine. Just as English sentences make up the English language, the instructions in the program make up the machine's language. This "machine language" is the most primitive and lowest level computer language, but even today it is here that programming starts. In 1950 it was the only language that could be used to prepare problems for computers.

The machine language is purely numeric, making it very difficult for a human to read and understand. It is even harder to read if it is written in the computer's favorite number system, the binary that just uses the digits 0 and 1. In his book on the history of computers, Goldstine illustrates this point by showing the code or program for the IAS machine that would calculate the simple formula:

C = A + B + AB (C equals A plus B plus A times B)

It takes seven instructions stored in the addresses numbered 0 through 6 to perform the required steps:

0. 00000010101111001010
1. 00000010111111001000
2. 00000011001110101000
3. 00000010101111001100
4. 00000010111111100010
5. 00000011001111001000
6. 00000011001110101000

Even if you had a code book telling what these long strings of ones and zeroes stood for, it would be tedious to translate them into normal English. It would be too great a task even for a skilled programmer to write a program of any length directly in numeric machine language. So the first thing that was done to make it easier was to go back to the method used in earlier computers and first write the program using letters and decimal numbers. Then the programmer would carefully translate the program into machine language. This helped the initial preparation, but did not relieve the programmer of the task of finally writing out those long binary numbers. Everyone realized that the programmer would be more productive if relieved of this heavy burden, so they programmed the computer to make the conversion from letters to numbers. But this seems like a contradiction when we have already said that a computer can only understand numbers.

The whole thing is possible when you remember that letters, decimal numbers and special symbols can be represented by a binary number or code. We have already encountered the teletype code and the standard ASCII code. Thus all we have to do is to code the letters and numbers into ASCII codes and they can be put in the computer's memory. A program can then be written in machine language to take these number representations of the programmer's letters and change them to the machine's language. This program is called an "assembler" and the new language that it understands is called the "assembly language." The programmer can write a program using the English letters and decimal numbers that we are all familiar with and the computer can figure out all the ones and zeroes. This assembly language is the next most easily understandable or next "higher" language for all modern computers.

However, even assembly language did not exist in the early days and the programmers worked hard to organize their machine language programs into small working units called subroutines. These subroutines consisted of operations that could be universally applied to many problems. Libraries of these subroutines were created and they could be inserted in the main program to save the labor of rewriting them many times.

The proceedings of the 1947 Harvard Symposium contain 302 pages, yet only 10 pages are enough to record the sixth session on "sequencing, coding, and problem preparation," or what we call software. Not that it was considered unimportant, but so little work had been done. That should not surprise us as there were still no stored program computers to try the programs out on. The two papers, one by Mauchly on the EDVAC type machines and one by Joseph Harrison on the preparation of problems for the Mark I Harvard calculator, did not even consider an assembly language, but concentrated on the idea of a library of subroutines. Mauchly addressed the problem of how to organize the subroutines in the memory of the EDVAC so they might be easily referenced as needed. Harrison did not concern himself with that problem as the Mark I was programmed with special "sequence" paper tapes and these were punched and placed in the machine at proper places. He did realize the extent of the programming problem and ended his paper with a paragraph in which he looked towards the future:

> Large-scale calculators in operation are beautiful instruments to observe. Their mechanical parts display craftsmanship; their electrical circuits show ingenuity; their over-all design indicates a high degree of organization. Nevertheless, their only excuse for being is to perform laborious mathematical calculations in a more economical manner. It seems, therefore, that one of the most important problems now facing us is to achieve a reduction in the preparation and set-up time proportionate to that reduction already achieved in the actual computation time.

With the first part of his statement, a modern computer engineer could be even more ecstatic. The beauty of the integrated circuit and the ingenuity, precision and craftsmanship of disk drives and keyboards surpass anything that computers had in 1947, not to mention the printed circuit boards and the beautiful full color pictures on the TV screens. Harrison's second observation, that computers exist only to do laborious calculations, has in the light of today's computer revolution, changed considerably. Both Turing and Von Neumann were the first to recognize that computers cannot only do arithmetic calculations, but they can also be logical machines that can work out problems by making decisions and playing games. They urged the early computer designers to build in instructions that could do logical operations like "or," "and" and "not." So although we do have computers that can make complex scientific and engineering calculations and some that can handle routine accounting jobs, we mostly use computers in other ways. We use them to get answers to questions, to help write letters and spell, to play games, to make decisions in the stock market and to automatically fly airplanes and rockets.

All these new computer applications have in large part come about through the development of new computer languages. These developments took place in the 1950s after the SWAC was built and the languages have names like FORTRAN, BASIC, PASCAL and C+. Called compilers, they let the programmer instruct the computer by writing formulas and logical operations using standard mathematical symbols and English language instructions. These languages, unlike ordinary English, are very precise and logically consistent. They are the next higher languages after machine and assembly languages.

Programmers use the compilers to make the programs that we all use to do our tasks. These are called application programs and work only for the specific task they are designed for, whether it be accounting, word processing or playing games. Application programs sometimes have the feature that they can be changed by those who use them to adapt to one's special problem. But to really change these programs, the programmer must use the language of the compiler that they were written in. The compilers allow the programmer to write new programs without necessarily knowing anything about how the computer is built or how it works. Many languages are understood by many types of computers and skilled programmers can talk to any one of them using one of these languages.

From the modern programmer's point of view a computer becomes an entity in itself and the programmer need not have any knowledge of the hardware or the machine language. Just as when we talk to a friend, we can communicate intelligently in a common language and don't need to understand the physiology of our bodies or how our brains work. If you can talk to a computer and like a friend, the computer can talk back to you, then does a computer think?

As we saw when our story began, Huskey was in England where he met and worked with the gifted English mathematician, Alan Turing. Of course, Turing was instrumental in the design and building of the ACE computer at the National Physical Laboratories. In 1950, Turing wrote a paper on the question that we just asked, can a machine think? He proposed a simple test for a computer and if the computer passed this test, he would then be convinced that a computer could indeed think. Of course he described his test in terms of the computers of the day, but I will describe his idea using today's technology.

Imagine that your personal computer was hooked up to a network of computers, like Internet. The network allows you to talk to others on their computers so you can have a conversation with them using your keyboard and video screen. The network also allows you to talk to a computer that may be programmed, for example, to give answers to questions like an encyclopedia. You can choose whether to talk to your Internet friend or to the computer and you know which it is you are connected to at any one time. But suppose that a friend of yours that's not acquainted with the network walks up to see what you are doing on your computer. You tell the friend that you are communicating with both a person and a computer, but you don't say which is the person and which is the computer. You then let your friend use your keyboard to talk to them. How long do you think it would take for your friend to find out which was which? Without taking the person's or computer's word for what they really were, all your friend can do would be to ask questions and get answers.

This is basically what Turing planned to do in his test. The computer was not to be programmed to operate like an automated encyclopedia but was to be cleverly programmed to simulate a person. The computer was to act as much as it could to make your friend believe it was a person. For example, when your friend asked for the answer to a math problem, the computer would have to take a long time to reply just as a person would do. In Turing's test your friend would have a fixed time to find out which is which. If you conducted the experiment many times with many friends and they guessed that the machine was a human as often as they guessed that the machine was a machine, then Turing would call the machine intelligent, concluding that it could think.

This is a very interesting idea and it has caused many heated controversies between philosophers and proponents of artificial intelligence. Some would accept Turing's definition of an intelligent machine, while others don't believe that a computer could ever think. Turing thought that by the end of the century a properly programmed computer could pass his test. Even if by then computers couldn't pass his test, he expected that they would have become so smart that the average person would rate them intelligent. It is of course, a fact that we blame our errors on the "dumb" computer and praise the workings of the "smart" computer that gives sensible answers. So we must be getting used to the idea that computers think, if only in their limited way.

There's a branch of computer science called artificial intelligence (AI), which tries to find ways to make computers more intelligent so they can help us more in day to day problems. Among the intelligent things that computers can do today, besides playing an excellent game of chess, are recognizing printed text, solving word problems like we had in algebra, finding proofs to theorems like those in geometry, helping doctors diagnose diseases from symptoms and helping musicians compose their music.

When the junk man asked Huskey for the weight of the SWAC, he was seeing the machine from his point of view. Today we have an almost unlimited number of ways to see a computer. The hardware engineer sees the integrated circuits. The programmer sees the operations of the program. The librarian sees an electronic card catalog. The educator sees a teaching machine. The mathematician sees a problem solver. The astronaut sees a pilot and navigator. Perhaps later in the 21st century people will see computers as intelligent beings.

GROWING UP 

The Dedication announced the birth of the SWAC and it was now time for careful nurturing of the machine so it could grow into a reliable and useful computer. There remained the small problems that were overlooked in the rush to get enough working for the demonstration on Dedication Day. Now these could be attended to carefully and the machine more finely tuned. Then the programmers could take over and finally do what the SWAC was created for—solving problems.

Dr. Melkanoff was one of the early physicists who programmed for the SWAC. In his talk for the Pioneer Day Session at the National Computer Conference in 1978, he recalled his introduction to the SWAC. When he first came to the INA, he was working on his Ph.D. thesis, which involved numerical methods to solve 13 by 13 matrices, a problem that has many scientific applications. He had started with mechanical calculators and then used the

IBM Card Programmed Calculator (CPC) which was housed near the INA computer room. He had hardly gotten the CPC programmed when he found out that it was being returned to IBM next week.

As he relates in his talk, "Then I was told 'It's all right, you can now go on to SWAC.' I said, What's that? They said, 'the computer in the next room.' It was an introduction I still recall. I was given, by one of the programmers, Ruth Horgan, a sheet of so-called documentation which primarily consisted of one page of thirteen instructions plus a notebook which I looked at several times but was never quite sure whether it was written in English or some other language."

So he and others had to program using the SWAC's thirteen instructions, that is, in machine language. One can't get any more basic than that. They checked or "debugged" their programs by using the step-by-step push buttons on the SWAC console and reading numbers from the neon lamps. These lamps were arranged in eight groups of four for the 36 bits of the SWAC word, plus an extra lamp for the 37th bit which represented the sign of the number. Each group of four bits can represent numbers up to 16 so the programmer could read each group of four lamps as a hexa-decimal or base 16 digit. The hexa-decimal representation became common in machine language programming. The 16 values of each digit are represented by the numerals 0 through 9 plus the letters A through F. So a SWAC number in hexa-decimal was nine digits long and might look like this when recorded by the programmer: +1A45BF19C.

In order to check a result of an arithmetic operation to see if the program was working correctly, the programmer would from time to time check the results.

Melkanoff tells us that adding in hexa-decimal was not so bad, but multiplication and division became a "bit of a problem." A bit of a problem for a mathematician but an almost impossible problem for the rest of us.

When they found an error, they would of course, report it to the engineers, who generally tried to blame the programmer by saying "maybe the program is wrong." And of course, many times the program was wrong but the error could also be caused by such a mundane hardware failure as a burnt out neon lamp on the console. Some programmers became so familiar with the hardware that they could sometimes fix problems themselves. The SWAC had a full complement of spare chassis and once the programmer had been able to pin-point the fault, all he had to do was unplug the bad chassis and use the spare. As Melkanoff describes it from the programmer's point of view:

> The chassis were fiendishly designed things as far as we were concerned. There were special tools to remove them, but they never quite fit, so you had to sit against the machine and pull them with both hands, bracing yourself against the thing and pulling with all your might until finally it came. Removal, however, was easy compared to returning the beasts themselves, because in addition to the dangers, the difficulty of putting them in, was the delightful crunch which you sometimes heard as you put it in, which still brings sweat to my brow.

With the engineers working during the day, the programmers were given the night shift. They even brought in a cot to sleep on while the SWAC was computing. The SWAC was rigged with a loudspeaker that was hooked up so the programmer could "listen" to the execution of the commands in his problem. If the computer performed add and subtract commands, a high note was produced. If the instructions occurred less often, a lower note would be produced. The programmer came to know the sounds that his program made and if he was lying on the cot resting, he would immediately know something went wrong when the pitch and rhythm of the sounds changed. By careful programming, the SWAC could be made to play a rudimentary tune and a program for generating random numbers produced a sequence of tones that was christened "random symphony."

Besides the prime number problem mentioned earlier, the SWAC, with its memory of only 256 words, did useful work in nuclear physics, optics, crystallography and meteorology. The programs had to make every word count. Melkanoff recalls that if he was able by hard work to save just one word, he would have a drink on the way home to celebrate. Then, finally, the memory was expanded by adding a magnetic drum.

Even as far back as the invention of the Stored Program Concept, von Neumann realized that a computer should have a hierarchy of memories. A fast electronic memory was necessary to take advantage of the stored program, but it was naturally limited by cost and would have to be served by a larger, slower and less expensive memory. It still is with your personal computer, which has three major memory devices: the high-speed solid-state "RAM" (Random-Access Memory), the hard disk and the much slower floppy disks. At the beginning, the only other memory that the SWAC had besides the Williams Tubes was punched-paper tape. Later a punched card reader and punch were added. These paper tapes and cards were not really a memory in the sense that the computer could read or write a word at any address. The computer could only read a tape or card, or write on a different tape or card. But programs and results could be stored on the tapes. The program and input data were read into the computer from cards or tape and the output data were stored by punching holes into other cards or tape.

Huskey knew the programming limitations caused by having only 256 words in electronic memory, so he had planned to add a magnetic drum to the SWAC. Magnetic drums were the forerunners of today's hard disks. The drums recorded the data as magnetic spots around the circumference on many separate tracks. Your personal computer's hard disk similarly records on tracks on the surface of a disk. The old drums were the magnetic analogy of the old Edison phonograph cylinders, while today's disks are analogous to the old LP phonograph record.

The design of magnetic drums was well known in 1950 since many computer projects, including Aiken's Harvard Mark III, used magnetic drum storage. The SWAC drum had 4000 37 bit words of memory, or somewhat less than 25,000 bytes. Not very much by today's standards, but it was almost 16 times more than the Williams tubes. During the construction of the SWAC, there was neither time nor money to build a drum memory, so it was left until after the Dedication.

In 1951 the magnetic drum project really got underway when Dr. R. Thorensen joined the SWAC staff. Thorensen's first job was to improve the reliability of the SWAC. So he made improvements in the hardware, replaced some of the early crystal diodes with more reliable tubes and improved the memory electronics. At the same time he designed and built the magnetic drum. The drum had a new feature—a single recording head was used for recording and playback. Up to then, like in your audio cassette player, a separate recording head was used for recording and playback. The drum had a recording head for each track and because there were 128 tracks, the new design really paid off by cutting the number of heads in half. Each head had to be carefully adjusted so that a small gap remained between it and the drum's surface. Needing an additional 128 heads would have made this task twice as difficult and would have significantly increased the cost of the drum memory.

The transfer of data from the drum to the memory was also done in a novel way. Each track stored 32 words and the circuitry was arranged so that all 32 words from one track could be transferred at high speed to the Williams tubes. This type of transfer was later called "direct memory access" (DMA), and is now used in all of today's disk memories. It gave the programmer immediate fast access to multiples of 32 words at a time, a real benefit to programmers who had only 256 words to use.

By 1953, the drum was operating and Huskey reported that the SWAC spent an average of 53.2 hours a week computing. Some problems only took minutes to solve while others took hundreds of hours.

The mathematicians continued to look for high prime numbers. The particular primes that the SWAC looked for are called Mersenne numbers, which are calculated by the formula 2^p-1. That is, 2 raised to the p power minus 1 in which p is a known prime number. For example, if p equals 3, then the Mersenne number is 2 cubed (2^3), or 8 minus 1 which equals 7, a prime. But all Mersenne numbers are not prime and must be tested to see if they can be divided by a different number than themselves and

1. The first few prime Mersenne numbers, when p is equal to 2, 3, 5, and 7, are 3, 7, 31 and 127. As p gets larger, the numbers get bigger very quickly and testing to see if they are prime also gets longer. After 453 hours, SWAC found a prime with p equal to 2281, which when written down would be over 700 decimal places long!

Scientists from the chemistry department at UCLA used the SWAC to analyze X-Ray diffraction patterns of crystals. This analysis allowed them to determine the arrangement of atoms inside the crystals. This is the same technique that Rosalind Franklin used in 1953 that led Nobel Prize winners James Watson, Francis Crick and Maurice Wilkins to discover the molecular structure of DNA. But they didn't have the SWAC to help them.

SWAC was also used for the study of the circulation patterns in the Earth's atmosphere with application to weather forecasting. This problem required the input of large amounts of data which was read in on punched cards. Altogether some 750,000 numbers were fed into the SWAC from punched cards during the course of the calculation. The entire problem took SWAC 325 hours to solve.

Famous mathematicians spent time at INA and developed new methods of numerical analysis. A new method for the solution of algebraic linear equations was developed by Lanczos and others. It was perfected by numerical tests on the SWAC. There were also many other problems in the fields of statistics, algebra and differential equations that were solved by the SWAC. Some of these added to the knowledge of numerical analysis, while others had practical engineering and scientific applications.

In 1954 NBS withdrew its support for INA and the SWAC was dismantled and re-erected in the Engineering Building at UCLA. It continued to operate until December

1967, when it was shut down for the last time. It was then 17 years old, the oldest of the early computers in operation. It had taken 18 months from conception to birth and a further three years to grow its magnetic drum. It had shown what a stored-program computer could accomplish with a high-speed parallel electronic memory and a simple instruction set. Although it seemed at times to be in the "backwater" of computer history, by the time of its retirement it had made a significant contribution to the computer revolution.

THE SWAC & THE PC

With only 256 words (about 1200 bytes) of memory, the SWAC was really limited to calculating one problem at a time. Like astronomers using a telescope, the programmers requested time, so each one would get on the schedule to run his or her problem alone. Of course many programs were the creation of a joint effort by more than one mathematician. Even so, it was usual to find a single programmer at the console or having a cup of coffee or playing cards while listening to the program run over the loudspeaker.

Thus the SWAC might well have been called a personal computer, as it was available to be used by one person at a time. Although your personal computer can indeed run many programs simultaneously, we call it a "personal" computer (PC) because it's for you alone. The modern programs allow a person with a minimum of training to use the computer, while on the other hand, the SWAC programmers were skilled mathematicians and programmers. Yet there is a similarity between the operation of the two computers and this similarity runs much deeper than its "personal" nature.

As we have seen, the SWAC had a high-speed electronic memory, a larger but slower magnetic drum memory and it processed the bits in its numbers and instructions in parallel. This parallel operation is the way computers work today and is taken for granted by computer scientists. Nowadays computer scientists use "parallel operation" to refer to a special computer that processes many instructions at one time or a system with many computers all working at once. That is not the way your usual PC works, but your computer does add all the bits in a number at once in its Arithmetic Logic Unit (ALU). In this the SWAC and the PC share common ground. The parallel arithmetic unit gave the SWAC the speed to be the fastest computer in its day. This same feature gives your PC the ability to operate at even faster speeds.

The SWAC's Williams tube memory stored its numbers and instructions as electric charges on the face of a TV tube. The solid-state random-access memory (RAM) in your PC stores the numbers as electronic charges on microscopic electronic capacitors in the integrated circuit memory chips. Both memories must be continuously refreshed so they won't forget. The data in the William's tubes was lost when the SWAC was shut down as is the data in your PC's RAM. After turning the power on again, the programs must be read from the hard or floppy disk. Similarly the SWAC had to be started from its magnetic drum or paper tape memories. Of course, it wasn't so easy to turn the SWAC on and off, so it usually ran all the time. It's somewhat consoling to know that when you feel a little foolish trying to remember a telephone number by repeating it to yourself that even with the latest technology, computers all over the world have to have their memories refreshed.

The arithmetic logical unit (ALU) in the latest PCs operate with 32 bit binary numbers. The SWAC had 37 bits. The ALU receives instructions from the RAM as the program is executed and like the SWAC, does one instruction at a time. The number of different instructions that it can perform differ for each type of PC. You will remember that Huskey wanted the number of instructions to be kept small. Yet in the 13 SWAC instructions, there were not only those that performed arithmetic, but also those that did logical operations like "or" and "and." During his visit to England, Huskey had heard Turing emphasize the need for a computer to have the ability to do logic. By doing logic the computer can be programmed to make decisions. Thus the SWAC control, unlike many earlier computers, was designed with logical instructions. And like the most modern PCs that use the latest RISC or "Reduced Instruction Set Control," the SWAC had a small but powerful instruction set.

Where the SWAC differed most from your PC was in size. It was not only physically bigger, but its memory capacity was smaller. Yet "all" one would have to do to make it work like a PC would be to add a few megabytes of solid-state memory, a few hundred megabytes of hard disk, a CRT color display and most importantly, the modern software. It was difficult enough to use machine language to create programs for the SWAC using less than 256 words (about 1200 bytes), but it would be impossible to use machine language to create the modern programs that contain 100,000 bytes or more. These programs had to await the development of software languages, assemblers and compilers.

The physical size of the SWAC, which weighed over a ton, was necessarily due to the electronic technology of its day. The small size of your desk or lap top computer is the result of the invention of the transistor and integrated circuit. Fifty years ago, no one dreamed that such an enormous size reduction would be possible. Computers would always be "giant brains," enormous in size and complexity, and therefore housed in large rooms. In fact it was predicted that perhaps four computers would satisfy the calculating requirements of the entire nation.

But despite the fact that the SWAC was large in size and deficient in memory, it had all the same elements as your PC. Both work in the same manner as von Neumann described in his 1944 report. They both go carefully through their memories looking for instructions and executing them one at a time. Some have called them "von Neumann Machines," because he had suggested this serial, one by one, processing. Both the SWAC and the PC have perhaps the most important thing in common, the Stored Program Concept.

The Stored Program Concept is what makes a computer. Whether it's large and clumsy like the SWAC, or small and efficient like your PC, every computer since 1945 has used this same important concept. It gave us the computer revolution.

The industrial revolution produced machines that relieved the human race from physical labor and later provided mechanical power beyond that required just to replace human muscle. Machines were made to move hundreds of tons of dirt at a time, forge red hot steel ingots, fly us at supersonic speeds and put man on the moon. Machines made the telegraph practical and later made the telephone, TV and communication satellites. Edison's gramophone has evolved into your hi-fi stereo. Still photography led to movies and then to television. Your PC is at first sight, just another addition to this long line of modern inventions that make our lives easier. Your computer does not appear to be much different from your TV, adding machine, hand calculator, wristwatch, toaster, refrigerator or for that matter, any other of a host of machines. It seems to be just another gadget to help us do certain mathematical tasks and to amuse us by playing games. But really it's more than that.

The computer is more than any other machine could hope to be. It's not just another machine; the revolution it created is unlike any other technological revolution since the beginning of civilization. The computer revolution cannot be compared to the industrial revolution, the transportation revolution started by Henry Ford's Model T or the communication revolution produced by TV and satellites. The computer revolution goes above and beyond these because the computer itself is more than just the sum of its parts, its performance more than what the designers of hardware and software make it do.

You might be tempted to say, "Isn't my computer only going to do what it was programmed to do? If it's programmed to do my bank balance, I sure hope it doesn't suddenly start doing something else." Well, it no doubt won't stray from its programmed path and will always do your bidding. But the computer may tell you that your checking account is overdrawn and surely the programmer didn't program it to always come up with that bad news. When the SWAC was programmed to find new large prime numbers, there was no way of predicting how long it would take and how big the prime number would be. The SWAC found prime numbers faster than its programmers ever could. If they knew in advance the values of the prime numbers, they would not have used the SWAC to find them and you wouldn't have used a computer program to balance your bank account if you already knew it was balanced.

Lady Lovelace, Charles Babbage's patron and collaborator on the Analytical Engine, believed that the engine could do no more than the operator instructed it to do. She was the first to say, "Computers can only do what you tell them to do." But computers do more than you tell them to do in another sense than getting the unknown balance on your checking account. For example, when a computer is programmed using a high-level language or compiler, the programmer isn't really directly telling the computer what to do. The compiler changes the programmer's program into the machine language that the computer understands. The programmer does not need to know the machine language and indeed, each make of computer has its own language. The machine language, the details of the computer's instructions and the operation of the ALU and memory are all hidden from the programmer's view. Just as when you use a word processor, you are not even aware of the thousands of instructions the computer is processing. The same thing happens when you eat a sandwich. You don't have to give your body instructions to digest your food. Your body, like the word processor, starts working automatically and it's not necessary for you to be aware of the internal workings of your digestive organs.

A third, more powerful way in which a computer can do more than it is made to do is illustrated by a game playing program written by Arthur Samuel, an early computer programmer. In 1950 he wrote a program to play checkers and he programmed his computer so it would make its move based on two criteria. First, it would look ahead and evaluate each possible move and what the effect would be several moves later. This took a long time for his 1950 computer, as there are many possible moves for each arrangement of pieces on the board. So Samuel combined this method with a no-look-ahead scheme that used a mathematical formula to calculate the best move from the known positions of the pieces. As the computer played, it compared the results of the long look-ahead method with that of the quick no-look-ahead method and adjusted the latter to make it give better results. This caused the computer to improve its play, eventually "learning" to play as well as the top checkers players in the world. It was a real achievement for Samuel as the success of the program relied on his insights into what checkers is, how the game is played and how to program a computer.

The "computers-only-do-what-you-tell-them-to-do" people said that the program only reflected Samuel's own skill in checkers. But the computer went on to beat Samuel at his own game and became a better checker player than he. In this way it did more than Samuel set out to do.

Your TV set can't improve on a poorly written soap opera. Your refrigerator can't improve on its ability to freeze foods. But the computer can give you unexpected answers and beat programmers at their own game. It does more than we would predict from the sum of its parts. It can do more because it stores its programs in memory and can modify its own instructions. The Stored Program Concept gave it this ability to change its own programs, to loop through subroutines and to do loops within loops within loops. The result is the first machine that can truly modify itself.

For 50 years we have had these self-modifying machines and now almost everyone has one on the desk at home or at the office. They will always be there to help us play games, analyze problems, make decisions and plan our work. These tasks are now so commonplace we take them for granted. And in the future, the computer will do even more tasks than we can now imagine.

The SWAC, its contemporaries, the modern PC and all computers that have been made, use the same organization and principles invented 50 years ago. These principles have given us the first self-modifying machines and were invented by three men. These three men started the computer revolution by inventing the Stored Program Concept. We should all remember them whenever we see or use a computer. They were, in alphabetical order,

J. Presper Eckert, Jr.
John Mauchly
and
John von Neumann.

APPENDIX 1:
THE METHOD
OF DIFFERENCES

Suppose you had lost your pocket calculator but needed a table of numbers and their squares to look up areas or figure the number of tiles it takes to tile a kitchen counter. You will remember that the square of a number is the result of multiplying the number by itself. The following is a list or table of the numbers 1 through 9 and their squares:

Number	Square
1	2
2	4
3	9
4	16
5	25
6	36
7	49
8	64
9	81

If you continued on with the table of squares, the multiplication would obviously become more difficult. So the mathematicians have given us a way of finding the squares by simply doing addition without having to multiply. Their "method of differences" is most easily explained by again showing our table of squares with additional columns to list the "differences":

Number	Square	Differences		
		First	Second	Third
1	1			
		3		
2	4		2	
		5		0
3	9		2	
		7		0
4	16		2	
		9		0
5	25		2	
		11		0
6	36		2	
		13		0
7	49		2	
		15		0
8	64		2	
9	?			

The first number in the first difference column shows the result of subtracting the square of 2 from the square of 1 or 4 minus 1. The next number in that column shows the difference between the square of 3 and the square of 2 or 9 minus 4. As we go down the column of squares, we continue to subtract the value of each square from the previous one. The second difference column shows the result of the same operations on the values in the first difference column, and lastly, the differences of the second differences are shown in the third difference column.

The unexpected result of these difference calculations is that all the second differences are 2 and all higher differences are zero. Now, if we want to continue our table of squares and find the square of 9 without multiplying 9 times 9, all we have to do is add 2 to the last first difference—15—and get 17, which we add to 64 to get 81, the correct result. And we can continue taking differences and adding to get the square of as large a number as we wish, and we don't have to multiply.

APPENDIX 2:
THE SWAC
ARITHMETIC UNIT

The Whirlwind used binary numbers only 16 bits long, while SWAC was to use 37 bits. Serial machines like the SEAC, EDVAC and UNIVAC used only one adder to add binary numbers as they came from their mercury delay line memories. As each digit was added, any carries that might occur were stored momentarily and later added to the next digit. The SWAC had 37 adders that added all the digits at once. But after adding all the digits, the carries had to be taken care of. The carry from each digit must be added to the sum of the next digit and if that resulted in a carry, it too must be added to the next digit and so on for 37 digits. Thus the carry signal cascaded or rippled down through the 37 adders. The addition wasn't finished until all the carries had been passed through all the adders. This carry propagation time was the critical time in the SWAC adder design, as every small delay in each adder would contribute 37 times to the total addition time.

In order to make a vacuum tube logic circuit fast, one has to make it use more power. Lacey had to use some very powerful tubes in order to obtain the necessary speed, but he managed to produce an adder that would give the SWAC an addition time of 5.7 microseconds. A single cycle of the SWAC clock, 8 microseconds, was the time allowed for adding two numbers, so Lacey's design was well within that limit and allowed for variations in the tubes.

As in the long multiplication you did at school, binary multiplication consists of multiplying the first number by every digit of the second number, placing each such partial product over to the left and adding them all. In binary multiplication we are dealing with only 1s and 0s, so the multiplication step is easy, but a 37 bit number still requires 37 adds. Lacey's adder could make 37 additions in 296 microseconds, while the original Whirlwind took 187 microseconds for only 16 bits and the SEAC took almost 3000 microseconds.

APPENDIX 3:
THE SWAC WILLIAMS TUBE MEMORY

In your TV the picture is produced by an electron beam in the TV tube that rapidly scans across and down the screen. The beam causes the TV screen to glow or fluoresce to produce the picture that you see. The glow rapidly fades so the beam has to scan the whole picture 30 times a second to produce a steady picture. In addition to the visible picture, the beam also produces an invisible pattern of electric charges on the TV screen.

The electron beam in the SWAC memory TV tubes was made to scan just the dots and dashes. Williams used a slightly different scheme for storing the binary numbers in the tube he made in England. In his tube, the electron beam scanned a single line across the face of the tube. Instead of dividing the whole screen into square cells, as was done in the SWAC memory, Williams divided the line into short pieces. 1s and 0s were represented by producing either a line (electron beam turned on) or a gap (electron beam turned off) in each cell.

In order to sense the stored pattern, Williams utilized the electric charge pattern on the face of his tube. He placed a copper window screen on the front of the tube's screen and hooked it up to a sensitive electronic amplifier. He found that the electric charge produced by scanning the line induced a signal on the copper screen. But like the picture on your TV, the electric charge along the line would fade unless the TV signal kept repeating it over and over. Williams found that the signal was different for a solid line than a gap, that is, between a 1 and a 0. In fact, even before the electron beam reached the gap, a signal was produced that anticipated a gap. Williams rigged the TV tube so when the amplifier sensed that a gap was coming up, the TV signal would reproduce the gap. The pattern on the face of the tube would then remain stable, storing the binary numbers.

Huskey modified this scheme to produce the dots and dashes on the SWAC memory tubes. Just like Williams' tube, each of the SWAC's 37 tubes was fitted with a copper screen on its face and a sensitive amplifier. As the dots and dashes were produced, like Williams' gaps they produced an electric signal on the copper screen which were amplified by the amplifier. The electrical signal from the amplifier again anticipated whether there was a dot or a dash.

So the SWAC memory tubes repeatedly scanned the dots and dashes and when the amplifier sensed a dot, it would immediately put a dot back onto the screen. When it sensed a dash, it would put a dash back onto the screen. So once the original pattern of dots and dashes was established, it would remain stored as spots of electric charge on the face of the TV tube.

The SWAC was a synchronous machine. It was timed by an electronic "clock" that produced 125,000 electric pulses a second. These pulses were used to sequence the operations of the computer, including the memory. The interval between pulses, 8 microseconds, was called a "half-cycle," a cycle being the interval between every other pulse, 16 microseconds. During the course of a clock cycle, the first half-cycle was used to write a bit (1 or 0) as a dash or dot in one memory cell. Since there were 37 memory cells, the 37 bits of a SWAC word were written at once. It took a similar time to read a memory cell. During the second half-cycle, each memory cell was refreshed, starting with cell 1 through cell 256. Thus it took 256 cycles, 4096 microseconds, to refresh all the memory cells.

APPENDIX 4:
THE SWAC INSTRUCTION

The SWAC instruction was 36 bits long. Four bits were used for the code that specified the instruction to be performed. A total of 32 bits were used by four 8-bit addresses. The 37th bit of the SWAC word represented the sign of a number and was not used in the instruction. The 8-bit addresses specified locations of four of the 256 memory cells in the SWAC memory. Thus the SWAC instruction was referred to as a "four address" instruction. The first two addresses told the control where to get the two numbers involved in a calculation, add, subtract, multiply and so on. The third address specified where to put the answer and the fourth address was used to cause the computer to jump to a new address and start a new routine there. This jump happened in operations that compared the value of two numbers and provided the program control feature of the Stored Program Concept. The control also had the program counter, which would sequentially count through addresses unless a jump was called for. The SWAC would automatically process instructions from sequential memory addresses unless instructed otherwise. The program counter and jump or branch instructions are still components in modern computers.

Huskey's idea was to keep the instruction set as simple as possible and the 4-bit operation code, which could have coded for as many as 16 instructions, was used to specify only 13 SWAC instructions. The technical descriptions of the instructions, as they appeared in the SWAC manual, are shown in Table 3. The "extract" instruction performs a logical "AND" between each corresponding digits of the "extractor" and "extractee" and can shift the result.

TABLE 3

SWAC Instruction Set (from "Manual of SWAC Computing System," 1954)

Instruction	First Address	Second Address	Third Address	Fourth Address	Instructions/sec or Words/sec
ADD	Augend	Addend	Sum	NI if Overflow	15,625
ADD*	"	"	"	NI	15,625
SUBTRACT	Minuend	Subtrahend	Difference	NI if Overflow	15,625
SUBTRACT*	"	"	"	NI	15,625
MULTIPLY	Multiplier	Multiplicand	Rounded-Off Product	NI	2604
MULTIPLY*	"	"	"	NI	2604
PRODUCT	"	"	Most Significant Part	Least Significant Part	2604
COMPARE	Minuend	Subtrahend	Difference	NI if difference nonnegative	15,625
COMPARE*	"	"	Difference of absolute values	"	15,625
EXTRACT	Extractor	Extractee	Result	Specifies Shift	2604 to 5208
INITIAL INPUT	(Program Counter specifies destination)			Device	40 wds/sec
INPUT	Destination	(Drum)	(Drum Channel)	"	Drum 2000, Cards 16
OUTPUT	Source	"	"	"	Drum 2000, Cards 16

Note: NI denotes the address of the next instruction.

CHRONOLOGY

1942

August	Mauchly and Eckert submit their memo on electronic computers to the Moore School.

1943

April	ENIAC project is approved.

1944

July	Huskey joins Mathematics Department at University of Pennsyvania
August	Goldstein meets von Neumann at Aberdeen railroad station.
September	Von Neumann's first visit to the ENIAC.
October	EDVAC project approved.

1945

April	Huskey starts part-time work on the ENIAC project.
June	Von Neumann's "First Draft of a Report on the EDVAC".
Fall	Turing joins NPL and begins ACE design.
November	Condon becomes director of the National Bureau of Standards (NBS).

1946

January	Travis becomes Supervisor of Research at Moore School.
February	ENIAC demonstrated to the public.
April	Eckert and Mauchly leave the Moore School.
June	Huskey resigns from the University of Pennsylvania.
July	Huskey accepts offer from the National Physical Laboratory.
December	Huskey goes to England.

1947

January	Huskey starts work at NPL.
May	UNIVAC named by Eckert-Mauchly.
July	The National Applied Mathematics Laboratories (NAML) set up by Condon. Consists of: The Institute for Numerical Analysis INA The Computation Laboratory Statistical Engineering Machine Development Laboratory, MDL
Fall	Williams has working model of his CRT memory.
October	Eckert-Mauchly get BINAC contract from Northrop.

1948

January	Huskey returns from NPL, England, and joins NAML.
March	NBS approves purchase of 3 UNIVACS from Eckert and Mauchly.
May 6	NBS decides to build their own computer. Huskey proposes a small machine to Curtiss.
May 18	SEAC project authorised by NBS.
May 24	Huskey gives two talks at Ohio State.
June 1	Huskey gave an address on "The Present State of Automatic Digital Computing Machinery" at the Association of Mechanical Engineers in Milwaukee.
July 29-31	Formal Opening of the INA. Second Symposium on Large-Scale Computing Machines. Huskey gives paper on "Programming for Machines Under Development."
October 19	SWAC project authorized.
December 6	Huskey arrives in Los Angeles.

1949

January	SWAC started at INA.
January 18	Lacey joins INA.
January 26	Ambrosio joins INA.
March 21	Rutland joins INA.
June	Two Symposia held at INA on subjects pertinent to the effective utilization of automatic digital computing machinery. Huskey gives paper "On the Definition of an Automatic Digital Computing Machine."
September 13	Huskey and SWAC engineers attend the Harvard Symposium and visit SEAC and Whirlwind. Huskey gives a paper on the "Zephyr" Computer (SWAC).
October	Huskey gives a course once a week on electronic computing machines.
December	SWAC 80 percent completed.

1950

April	NBS names SWAC and SEAC.
June 12	AIEE meeting in Pasadena. Huskey and Lacey gave papers on the SWAC.
June	SEAC Dedication.
August 17-18	SWAC Dedication.

1951

Fall	Thorensen joins the SWAC project.

1953

Magnetic Drum Operational.

1954

NBS withdraws support from INA.
SWAC moved to UCLA Engineering Building.

1967

SWAC, 17 years old, was finally dismantled.

FURTHER READING

The computer pioneers themselves gave papers on the history of their own projects at the International Research Conference on the History of Computing in 1976 at the Los Alamos Scientific Laboratory. These give first-hand accounts of all the early computer projects. They have all been compiled into one handsome volume:

Metropolis, N. C., J. Howlett, and Gian Carlo Rota. *A History of Computing in the Twentieth Century: A Collection of Essays.* New York: Academic Press, 1980.

Included are papers covering all the early machines in the U.S. and Europe and the development of software. The following papers bear directly on the subject of this book:

Bigelow, Julian. Computer Development at IAS Princeton: 308-9.

Burks, Arthur W. From ENIAC to the Stored-Program Computer: Two Revolutions in Computers: 311-342.

Backus, John. Programming in America in the 1950's: 125-135.

Eckert, J. Presper, Jr. The Eniac: 530-537.

Householder, A. S. Reminiscences of Oak Ridge: 386-387.

Huskey, Harry D. The National Bureau of Standards Western Automatic Computer: 419-431.

Wilkinson, J. H. Turing's Work at the National Physical Laboratory: 107-113.

The above papers and many of the books on the history of the early computers are made to be read by someone familiar with the operation and organization of both hardware and software. These books listed below cover the early history, but concentrate on the Eckert-Mauchly-Von Neumann story and unfortunately do not mention the SWAC.

Some of the less technical are:

Augarten, Stan. *Bit by Bit.* New York: Tucker and Fields, 1984.

Bowden, B. V., *Faster than Thought.* London: Pitman and Sons, 1953.

Wulforst, Harry. *Breakthrough to the Computer Age.* New York: Scribner, 1982.

Shurkin, Joel N. *Engines of the Mind: a History of the Computer.* New York: Norton, 1984.

Kidwell, Peggy A., and Paul E. Ceruzzi. *Landmarks in Digital Computing: A Smithsonian Pictorial History.* Washington: Institution Press, 1994.

More technical books on the history, but still without the SWAC story, are:

Ceruzzi, Paul E. *Reckoners: The Prehistory of the Digital Computer, from Relays to the Stored Program Concept, 1935-1945.* Westport: Greenwood Press, 1983.

Goldstine, Herman H. *The Computer from Pascal to Von Neumann.* Princeton: Princeton University Press, 1972.

Huskey, Harry D. Book Review: On the History of Computing by H. H. Goldstine. *Science* 180:588-590, May 11, 1973.

Nash, Stephen. *A History of Scientific Computing: ACM Conference on the History of Scientific and Numeric Computation (1987: Princeton, N.J.).* Reading: Addison-Wesley, 1990.

Ritchie, David. *The Computer Pioneers. The Making of the Modern Computer.* New York: Simon and Schuster, 1986.

Williams, Michael R. *A History of Computing Technology*. New Jersey: Prentice Hall, 1985.

Details of the SWAC and its performance are covered by the following papers given by Huskey and others on the SWAC team:

Huskey, Harry D. Electronic Digital Computing in the United States. In *The Early British Computer Conferences*, edited by Michael R. Williams et al. Cambridge: MIT Press, 1949:126-128.

_______ Characteristics of the INA Computer. *Mathematical Tables and Other Aids to Computation*. 4(30):103-108, 1950.

_______ The National Bureau of Standards Western Automatic Computer. In *A History of Computing in the Twentieth Century*, edited by N. Metropolis, J. Howlett, and Gian-Carlo Rota. New York: Academic Press, 1980:419-431.

Huskey, Harry D., E. Lacey, D. Rutland, and H. Larson. Design Features of the NBS Western Automatic Computer (digest). *Electrical Engineering* 69(8):723-724, 1950.

Huskey, Harry D., T. Larson, R. Thorensen, M. Melkanoff, and D.H. Lehmer. 1978. SWAC—Standards Western Automatic Computer. In *Transcript: Pioneer Day Session at the National Computer Conference*, edited by H. D. Huskey. Unpublished. July 1978.

Huskey, Harry D., R. Thorensen, B. F. Ambrosio, and E. C. Yowell. The SWAC—Design Features and Operating Experience. *Proceedings of the IRE* 41(10):1294-1299, 1953.

And the SWAC from the programmer's point of view:

Blanch, Gertrude and Ida Rhodes. Table-Making at the National Bureau of Standards. In *Studies in Numerical Analysis: Reprints in Honor of Cornelius Lanczos*, edited by B. K. P. Scaife. London: Academic Press, 1974:1-6.

Hestenes, Magnus R. and John Todd. NBS-INA—The Institute of Numerical Analysis—UCLA 1947-1954. *NIST Special Publication 730*. Washington, D.C.: National Institute of Standards and Technology, U.S. Department of Commerce, August 1991.

Lowan, A. N. The Computation Laboratory of the National Bureau of Standards. *Scripta Mathematica* 15:33-63, 1949.

Todd, John. Numerical Analysis at the National Bureau of Standards. *SIAM* 17:361-370, 1975.

And then there are the news reports on the SWAC:

Mark of Progress. *Time*, Sept. 4, 1950:56.

Mechanical Brain. *Los Angeles Examiner,* Aug. 18, 1950.

New Robot Brain Unveiled at UCLA. *Los Angeles Times,* Aug. 18, 1950.

Robot Knows the Score but can't Play. *Los Angeles Daily News,*
    Aug. 18, 1950.

Talking Zephyr. *Newsweek,* June 13, 1949:52.

UCLA Unveils New Brain. *Los Angeles Mirror,* Aug. 18, 1950.

The best source on the history of computers and contributions on the controversy on who invented the Stored Program Concept are the articles published since the early 1980's in the Annals of the History of Computing. The following papers are particularly interesting from the point of view of this book:

Aspray, William F. History of the Stored-Program Concept. *Annals of the History of Computing* 4(4):359-361, 1982.

Aspray, William and M. Gunderloy. 1989. Early Computing and Numerical Analysis at NBS. *Annals of the History of Computing* 11(1):8-9, 1989.

Gruenberger, F. J. The History of the JOHNNIAC. *Annals of the History of Computing* 5(2):213-217, 1979.

Huskey, Harry D. The National Bureau of Standards Western Automatic Computer (SWAC). *Annals of the History of Computing* 2(2):111-121, 1980.

________ From ACE to the G-15. *Annals of the History of Computing* 6(4):350-371, 1984.

Metropolis, N. and J. Worlton. A Trilogy of Errors in the History of Computing. *Annals of the History of Computing* 2(1):49-56, 1980.

Phelps, Byron E. Early Electronic Computer Developments at IBM. *Annals of the History of Computing* 2(3):253-267, 1980.

Stern, Nancy. John Von Neumann's Influence on Electronic Digital Computing, 1944-1946. *Annals of the History of Computing* 2(4):349-362, 1980.

________ Burks on the Stored Program Concept. *Annals of the History of Computing* 4(2):183-184, 1982.

________ The BINAC: A Case Study in the History of Technology. *Annals of the History of Computing* 1(1), 1979.

________ John William Mauchly: 1907-1980. *Annals of the History of Computing* 2(2):100-103, 1980.

Wilkes, Maurice W. Mauchly's Position on Von Neumann's Role in Drafting the EDVAC Report. *Annals of the History of Computing* 2(4):376-377, 1980.

The story of von Neumann's contribution to the Stored Program Concept is told in the following books and papers:

Aspray, William and Arthur W. Burks. *Papers of John von Neumann on Computing and Computer Theory: Charles Babbage Institute Reprint Series for the History of Computing,* Vol. 12. Cambridge: MIT Press; Tomash Publishers, 1987.

Aspray, William. *John von Neumann and the Origins of Modern Computing* of the *History of Computing Series.* Cambridge: MIT Press, 1990.

and, of course, von Neumann's famous First Draft Report:

Von Neumann, John. 1945. First Draft Report on the Edvac. in *Collected Works of Von Neumann* edited by A. H. Taub. MacMillan, 1961-1963.

More on the ENIAC and Eckert and Mauchly can be found in:

Campbell Kelly, Martin, and Michael Williams. *The Moore School Lectures: Theory and Techniques for Design of Electronic Digital Computers, 1944* of the *Charles Babbage Institute Reprint Series for the History of Computing,* Vol. 9. Cambridge: MIT Press; Tomash Publishers, 1985.

Mauchly, John W. Amending the Eniac Story. *Datamation,* Oct. 1979:217-220.

________ Preparation of Problems for EDVAC-TYPE Machines. In *The Proceedings of a Symposium on Large Scale Digital Calculating Machinery, 1947.* Cambridge: Harvard University Press, 1948:208-210.

Stern, Nancy B. *From ENIAC to UNIVAC: An Appraisal of the Eckert-Mauchly Computers.* Bedford: Digital Press, 1981.

________ *From ENIAC to EDVAC.* Bedford, Mass. Digital Press, 1981.

Tropp, Henry C. The Effervescent Years: A Retrospective. *IEEE Spectrum,* 11(4):70-79, 1974.

Another volume containing original papers covering the very

early period from the turn of the century to the ENIAC is:

Randell, Brian. *The Origins of Digital Computers: Selected Papers.* New York: Springer-Verlag, 1973.

Among others it contains a description by Atanasoff himself written in 1940:

Atanasoff, J. V. A Computing Machine for the Solution of Large Systems of Linear Algebraic Equations. In *The Origins of Digital Computers: Selected Papers,* edited by Brian Randell. New York: Springer-Verlag, 1973:305-310.

More information on Atanasoff is given in:

Aspray, William. *Computing before Computers.* Ames, Iowa: Iowa State University Press, 1990.

Burks, Alice R., and Arthur W. Burks. *The First Electronic Computer: the Atanasoff story.* Ann Arbor: University of Michigan Press, 1988.

The history of computers in England and Turing's contribution are to be found in:

Carpenter, B. E., and R. W. Doran. *A. M. Turing's ACE Report of 1946 and Other Papers,* Vol. 10, No. 10 of the *Charles Babbage Institute Reprint Series for the History of Computing.* Cambridge: MIT Press; Tomash Publishers, 1986.

Wilkes, M. V. *Memoirs of a Computer Pioneer.* Cambridge: MIT Press, 1985.

Williams, Michael and Martin Campbell-Kelley. *The Early British Computer Conferences,* Vol. 14 of the *Charles Babbage Institute Reprint Series for the History of Computing.* Cambridge: MIT Press; Tomash Publishers, 1989.

There have been many books on computer history over the last 50 years and if the reader is interested in more references the following work should be consulted:

Cortada, James W. *A Bibliographic Guide to the History of Computing, Computers, and the Information Processing Industry.* New York: Greenwood Press, 1990.

This thick volume lists the many references by subject and is a must for anyone doing research on the history of computers.

INDEX

ACM (Association for Computing Machinery), 108
Aerophysics Laboratory, North American Aviation, 17-20
Aiken, Howard, 35,142
Alexander, Samuel, 23
Alford, Brent, 27
Ambrosio, Biagio:
  joins SWAC, 26
  designs SWAC memory, 96-99
  constructing SWAC memory, 117
ASCII Code, *see* Numbers
Atanasoff, John, 45
Babbage, Charles, 32-35
Bell Telephone Laboratories:
  computer, 44, 47 (Table 1), 49
  trans-atlantic telephone, 91
Bigelow, Julian:
  and IAS machine, 86
  on cooperation with other projects, 111-112
Bits, *see* Numbers
Blanch, Gertrude, 106
Boelter, L. M. K., 24, 26
Brainerd, John Grist, 57
BRL (Ballistics Research Laboratory), 56
Burks, Arthur W., 59, 71
Bytes, *see* Numbers
Calculators:
  Babbage Difference Engine, 32-33
  Mechanical Desk, 31, 56
  Mental Arithmetic, 31-32
  Pascal's, 30, 31
Cannon, E. W., 24
Census, Bureau of, 22, 24
Cohn, Al, 26
Computer Design:
  early problems, 88, 90-91
  error checking, 88
  life of tubes, 87-88
  logical operations, 133
  parallel/serial operation, 85
  stored program machines, 88, 89 (Table 2)
  synchronous/asynchronous operation, 85-86
  vacuum tube circuits, 101
Computers, Analog, Differential Analyser, 56
Computers, by name:
  ACE, 12-14, 134
  Analytical Engine, 33-35, 47 (Table 1)
  ASCC, 35, 44, 47 (Table 1)
  AVIDAC, 82
  Bell Telephone Laboratories, 44, 47 (Table 1)
  BINAC, 62, 73, 78, 89 (Table 2)
  Control Data 6000, 82
  Difference Engine, 32-33
  DYSEAC, 82
  EDSAC, 68, 89 (Table 2)
  EDVAC, 78, 89 (Table 2), 132
  Harvard Mark I (ASCC), 35, 44, 47 (Table 1), 132
  Harvard Mark II, 45, 52, 47 (Table 1)
  Harvard Mark III, 142
  IAS Machine, 70-71, 89 (Table 2)
  IBM 360, 82
  ILLIAC, 82
  Iowa State, 45-46, 47 (Table 1)
  JOHNNIAC, 81-82, 86
  ORDVAC, 82
  RAYDAC, 82
  SILLIAC, 82
  UNIVAC, 82, 89 (Table 2)
  Whirlwind, 89 (Table 2), 90-91, 112
  Zuse Z3, 46-47 (Table 1)
  see also ENIAC, PC, SEAC, SSEC, SWAC
Computers, general:
  artificial intelligence, 136
  basic principles, 3
  checker program, 151-152
  computer revolution, 3, 150-153
  doing more than they are made to do, 150-152
  existing in 1947, 44-45

fiftieth Anniversary, 3
five basic operations, 30
invention of, 3-4, 72-73
inventors of, 94
naming of, 77-82
self modifying machines, 152-153
time to complete early machines, 122
Turing test, 134-136
unlike other machines, 2
Condon, E. U., 21
Curtiss, John, 22-24, 108
Differential Analyzer, 56
Differences, Method of, 32, Appendix 1
Dolmatz, Arnold, 27
Eckert, J. Presper:
  invents mercury delay line, 60-62
  life of, 58
  resigns from ENIAC project, 8
  and the stored program concept, 3, 153
Eckert and Mauchly:
  companies formed by, 73
  consider next machine, 59
  invent the stored program concept, 3, 62, 63
  receive NBS study contract, 22
  talks with von Neumann, 66-67
  views on computers, 69
  see also patents
Eidem, Blanche, 27
ENIAC:
  design characteristics, 44, 47 (Table 1)
  completion, 3
  engineering team, 59
  the Master Programmer, 53
  naming of, 78
  number of tubes, 83
Feldman, Sam, 24
Goldstine, Herman:
  at Executive Council meeting, 23
  at Moore School, 58
  circulates Draft Report, 68
  meets von Neumann, 64-66
  on modifiable addresses, 75
  von Neumann job offer, 71
Green, Sidney, 27
Gunning, William:

at RAND, 81
and SWAC memory, 97, 117
Harrison, Joseph, 132
Hartree, Douglas R., 8, 9
Harvard Symposium 1947, 43-44, 132
Householder, A. S., 109
Huskey, Harry D.:
  ACE, 12-14
  appearance on Groucho Marx show, 128
  arguments with Turing, 13
  assigned SWAC project, 25
  at Executive Council meeting, 24, 25
  Cambridge (Wilkes) offer, 15
  concept of SWAC, 4
  courses at INA, 107-108
  english computer projects, 14
  ENIAC experience, 7-8
  in England, 7, 10-12
  joins NAML, 22
  joins Moore School, 59
  leaves the University of Pennsylvania, 8
  life and education, 7-8
  meets Hartree, 9
  NBS job offer, 14, 15
  NPL job offer, 10
  returns from England, 20, 22
  and the stored program concept, 63
IBM, punched cards, 35
INA (Institute of Numerical Analysis):
  computer room, 29, 30
  education at, 108
  formation of ACM, 108
  mechanical calculators, 29, 30
  numerical analysis at, 106-107
  programmers at, 106
  reason for existence, 104-105
  symposia at, 106-107
  UCLA buildings, 28
Instructions:
  ENIAC Master Programmer, 53
  in stored program concept, 73-74
  in numerical form, 52-53
  used in SWAC, 99-100, Appendix 4
Lacey, Edward:
  joins SWAC, 26

designs SWAC arithmetic unit, 95-96

constructs SWAC arithmetic unit, 110-111

Lanczos, Cornelius, 107, 144

Larson, Harry, joins SWAC, 27

Lipkis, Roselyn Siegel, 27, 106

Lovelace, Lady Ada, 151

Luxemberg, Harold, 27

Magnetic Drums, 141-143

Maier, Oscar, 24, 25

Manchester University, 15

Markakis, Michael, 27

Marx, Groucho, 128

Mathematical Tables Project, established by WPA, 21

Mauchly, John:
  1942 memo on computers, 57
  life of, 56-57
  on programming, 132
  resigns from ENIAC, 8
  and the stored program concept, 3

Melkanoff, Michel, 138-140

Memory Devices:
  capacitor, 45
  mercury delay line, 61-62

Metropolis, N., 80

Moore School of Engineering (University of Pennsylvania):
  differential analyser at, 56
  ENIAC project, 7
  ENIAC contract, 58
  lectures, 9
  reports on digital circuits, 101
  see also Eckert, Mauchly, Goldstine, von Neumann

NAML (National Applied Mathematics Laboratory):
  authorizes SEAC, 23
  Executive Council meeting, 23, 24
  units of, 22

NBS (National Bureau of Standards):
  1950 census, 22
  computer study contracts, 22
  withdraws support of SWAC, 144-145
  see also NAML, INA

NPL (National Physical Laboratory, England), 6, 134

Newberger, John, 27

Numbers:
  ASCII code, 42
  bi-quinary, 40-41
  binary, 36-39
  bits, 40
  bytes, 42
  using fingers, 38-40

Numerical Analysis, 105

Oak Ridge National Laboratory, 109

Paper Tape, 41

Pascal, Blaise 30-31

Patents:
  Eckert and Mauchly, 76
  EDVAC denied, 72, 76
  ENIAC, 46, 69
  unpatentable inventions, 93-94

PC (Personal Computer), 4, 5, 86-87, 146-149

Phelps, Byron, 52

Prime Numbers, 143-144

Problems: solved on SWAC, 141, 143-144

Programming:
  assembly language, 131
  checking on SWAC console, 139-140
  compilers, 133-134
  early attempts, 131-133
  on ENIAC, 53-54
  use of loudspeaker, 140-141
  machine language, 129-131, 139
  on SWAC, 138-141

Programs:
  branch on sign, 51-52
  loops, 75-76
  discriminator, 49-51
  on paper tapes, 50, 52
  see also Instructions

RAND, 81

Raytheon, 22

RCA, 70

Rees, Mina, 24, 25

Rutland, David (author):
  at Aerospace, 17
  designs SWAC control, 99-102
  joins SWAC, 20, 27

Samuel, A., 151-152

SEAC:
  authorized, 23

delay lines used in SWAC, 112
architecture, 84-85, 89 (Table 2)
naming of, 79
Sharpless, T. Kite, 59
Shaw, Robert, 59
Siegel, Rosalind, *see* Lipkis
SSEC (IBM):
  characteristics of, 45, 47 (Table 1)
  numeric instructions in, 52-53
  branch on sign feature, 53-54
Stibitz, George, 49-51
Stored Program Concept:
  Eckert-Mauchly part in, 62-63
  importance of, 3, 73-76
  in PC, 4
  what makes a computer, 149-150
SWAC:
  and the PC, 4, 146-149
  architecture, 84-85, 89 (Table 2)
  arithmetic unit design, 95, 96, Appendix 2
  arithmetic unit construction, 110-111
  attenders to dedication, 125
  built by NBS, 4
  cabinet for (and air conditioning), 122-123
  chassis construction, 114-115
  control unit, 112-114
  control console, 123-124
  control console, operation, 139-140
  control unit design, 99-102, Appendix 4
  cooperation with other projects, 111-112
  dedication, 121-126
  design requirements, 25
  dismantled, 145
  finding errors, 140
  magnetic drum, 141-143
  memory design, 96-99, Appendix 3
  memory construction, 116-119
  memory flaws, 117-118
  naming of, 78-80
  NBS withdraws support, 144-145
  newspaper reports, 125-126
  number of tubes, 84
  oscilloscopes used in, 115-116
  personnel hired, 27

  problem in arithmetic unit, 120
  problems solved, 126-127
  project authorized, 25
  pulse transformers in, 112-113
  rack arrangement, size of, 119
  spare chassis, 140
  transferred to UCLA, 144-145
  uses Williams Tube, 25
  see also Programming
Tables, mathematical:
  firing and bombing, 55
  NBS role in, 21-22
Tektronix, 115-116
Thorensen, R., 142
Travis, Irven, 69
Tropp, Henry, 111
Turing, Alan:
  design of the ACE, 11-13
  Turing test, 134-136
Von Braun, Werner, 18-19
Von Neumann, John:
  and computers, 3, 81, 101, 133, 153
  association with RCA, 70
  draft report on EDVAC, 67-68
  hears of ENIAC, 64-65
  starts IAS machine project, 70-71
  life of, 65-66
  offer to Goldstine and Burks, 71
  offer to Eckert, 71-72
  views on computers, 69
  visits ENIAC, 66
  von Neumann machines, 149
Walsh, James, 27
Ware, Willis, 81
Wilkes, Maurice:
  at Moore School Lectures, 9
  receives draft report, 68
Williams, F. C., 15, 16, 118
Williams, Samuel, 49-51
Williams Tubes:
  as memory, 16, 142
  design of, 96-99, Appendix 3
  construction of, 116-119
Zuse, Konrad, 46-47

For extra copies of this book send $24.95
plus $3.00 postage and handling to:

Wren Publishers
PO Box 1084
Philomath, OR 97370

or call (503) 929-4498.